CRUSHING SUFFERING:

12 Ultimate Secrets
of **DEFEATING** Stress, Anxiety, Agony, Depression
and **INCINERATING** Tragedy

(With Extreme Survival Stories and Inspiring Life Quotes)

by William Thinh Than

This book is dedicated to all difficult lives out there. May courage and strength be always with you!

CONTENTS

INTRODUCTION

"Don't wish for a life that you can't have. But wish for the very life that you do own. And wish that you know how to make the most of it!"

Are you feeling tired, anxious, feared, stressed, depressed or lonely?

Have you encountered a crippling accident, experienced a terminal illness, or lost the love of your life?

Do you have friends or relatives who are in much trouble, stress and negativity that you'd like to assist their ways, ignite their hearts, and pull them out of dark days?

"Crushing Suffering" will help inspire your day and excite your way. It will walk with you in darkness. It will befriend your heart, lead you out of sufferings, and let you know how courageous you can really be.

Everybody has to deal with life's ups and downs, negative feelings and situations from time to time. No exception! Hate and anger, danger and worry, misery and distress, you can let them obsess your life and tear your soul apart. Or you can choose to fight hard and bounce back, and regain happiness from those dark days.

The choice is yours!

"Crushing Suffering" will help you:

- Overcome pain and grief, fear and stress, worry, anxiety and depression.

- Deal with difficult problems and difficult people.

- Take charge of every feeling and action.

- Fill up your energy and vitality.

- Regain your strength and happiness.

- Fall in love with your heart and your life.

- Revive the joy and passion of it.

- Inspire and excite this day to the utmost.

- Be your boldest self to challenge challenges, defeat difficulty and incinerate any ache that comes.

No matter how bad and how sad things have been to you, life will not be hopeless. No matter how much fear and stress, regret and worry, agony and mishap have afflicted your way, you'll not walk alone.

No matter what happens, I wish you a happy and fulfilling day ahead.

A New Life Is On!

1

THE MEANING OF LIVING THIS LIFE

To begin to think with purpose, is to enter the ranks of those strong ones who recognize failure as one of the pathways to attainment.

- James Allen

The mystery of human existence lies not in just staying alive, but in finding something to live for.

- Fyodor Dostoyevsky

The soul which has no fixed purpose in life is lost; to be everywhere, is to be nowhere.

- Michel de Montaigne

Listen to the whisper of your heart.

Hear your true self talking.

Have you planned your life out clearly?

Are you living with a purpose?

But eventually, you may ask, what's a purpose?

A purpose is, in fact, the ultimate calling of one's heart. A purpose is the very thing that motivates you to a greater height and a greater life. A purpose is the ultimate difference between a man and a walking corpse.

Without purpose, we might exist, but we'd never truly live.

Life's purpose, for some people, is their religion, their God. For others, it's their job, their family or their country. Alternatively, it may be their love for science, art, music, or their heart for fairness, freedom and world peace, or any other thing that brings meaning and excitement to their existence.

Enter the persistent will of Hiroo Onoda.

Mr. Onoda was a Japanese soldier who was dispatched to the island of Lubang in the Philippines to spy on the U.S forces. He remained persistently in the jungle for astonishingly 29 years, without believing in messages saying that the war had ended. During his extreme time surviving in the bush, he had to live on all kinds of food that he could gather from the forest and steal from the locals.

Onoda was finally persuaded by his former commanding officer and came out of the forest in 1974.

What kept Onoda alive and fight on for so many years, without any thought of surrender or killing himself?

His ultimate purpose was, in fact, the loyalty for his country. It was the crucial mission that he was given by the commanding officer. It kept him alive by giving him a great meaning to live on and fight on till his death.

Enter the tragic life of Blaise Pascal.

Pascal was a French mathematician, physicist, an inventor and a writer. His mother passed away when he was only three years old. From the age of eighteenth, Pascal was unfortunate to suffer from a serious nervous problem that left him hardly a day without agony. Sadly enough, he also went through a debilitating paralysis and depression later on. During those darkest days, nevertheless, Pascal made his name by producing many famous mathematical and physical works. His passion for science and the world ignited his heart, led him out of dark days and helped him make a difference.

A truly inspiring difference!

Pascal passed away on 19 August, 1662 in agony and convulsions, at the age of just thirty nine.

May he rest in peace!

YOUR HIDDEN POWER

So, after all, why do purposes really matter?

First and foremost, purposes show you the exact direction and destination of existing each day. Purposes give you the power to know exactly what is important and what is not. Without purposes, you're like a raft flowing aimlessly in the river of life, having no actual clue of what to do and what to lean on.

Importantly, purposes give you the fulfillment and meaning of living this life. A life without purposes is a life without ultimate meaning. Living without purposes is no different from living a life full of dissatisfaction and emptiness, of weariness and uncertainty.

What's more, purposes grant you life's precious energy and enthusiasm. A life with true purposes is a life with elation and excitement. It indulges you in the very action and makes you lose your sense of time. It's the very source of vitality that wakes you up in the morning, inflames your heart with passion, and keeps your night sleepless. It's the very origin of inspiration, aspiration and greater deeds.

And lastly, purposes bring you strength and courage during your hard times. Purposes help you climb on despite tired legs and hunger. Purposes help you turn persistent and resolute against all storms. Purposes are the reasons you can sacrifice all enticing pleasures for a bigger self. And purposes are the reasons why you can smile and thank for this life despite anything that hurts.

And as Nick Vujicic said: "I don't need arms and legs in this life, but I do need meaning and hope in an eternal life!"

So let every day be a chance to live with your true love and affection. Maybe it's your dear family or your meaningful job. Maybe it's your love for music and poems. Maybe it's your dream for stars and planets. Or perhaps, it's your wish to make others smile, bring peace to the Earth, or make this world a better place.

Every day is a chance to truly exist and march toward your dreams. Every day a chance to wake up with zeal and exhilaration!

Every second is a chance to shine and inspire your own heart. Every passing day is a chance to share smiles and liveliness to this world.

Each and every day, you have the chance to know your true heart. Each and every day, you have the chance to fall in love with this life.

Each and every day, you have the chance to live great, to make it all a difference!

And let your purposes be the arrow of life that pulls you forward. The more exciting and inspiring your purposes are, the tougher this arrow will get! Let it be relentless and unstoppable against all hurricanes. Let it penetrate every sadness and every darkness along your path. And let it aim right to the very heart of your fantastic life dreams.

Find out the arrow of your life, NOW! Let it destruct and crush any negativity that you're enduring. Let it ignite the positivity and liveliness of your own existence.

Love with all your heart!

And live with all your soul.

Indulge in the thirst for life. Indulge in the fire and passion of it!

Smile and long for each day as if it were the last.

THE VITAL QUESTIONS

Sometimes in life, you may catch yourself having no clue of what to do and what to lean on. You may get lost, bored, or you may get negative and depressed. This may be a sign that you don't know exactly what your true passions and purposes of life are. As such, you should explore yourself and find them out immediately. It's critical to do so.

You may ask yourself:

"If i had all the time, money and freedom needed, what would i do?

What makes me enjoy so much and lose my sense of time?

What would i live for or sacrifice for?

And what would a perfect day of mine look like?"

For a start, try out more activities and experiences in order to get a deeper understanding of your own mind. Realize what you love and what you don't. Recall the fire and excitement that you've forgotten since you were a child, and find out your true self!

After that, list out all passions and purposes of your life that you can possibly think of, and ponder upon them. Maybe there are various activities that you'd like to do. Maybe there are various things that you'd like to have. But recognize the true passions which set your life on fire, and find out the true purposes which ignite that flame of youth inside your heart.

A great secret for finding motivation in life is to connect whatever you've got to do or whatever you're going through to your ultimate purposes. Truly believe that your current situation would eventually give you invaluable courage, lessons, experiences and ultimately lead you to a fulfilling life path.

For instance, if your purpose in life is your dear family, genuinely believe that today's work and its troubles would ultimately serve your beloved ones. If your purpose in life is your faith in God, sincerely believe that every suffering would eventually show your dear God how courageous and skillful you are, and let him be truly proud of your heart. Assigning a purposeful meaning to every event and everything in life this way would give you a great meaning, courage, confidence and motivation to stride tirelessly forward.

So today, let's find out the meaning of everything in life.

Embrace our journey.

And have faith in our own path.

And crucially, be fully aware of our free time. It'd be best if we could plan those free hours for our passions and purposes, since having free time without knowing exactly what to do, or merely using it to pursue random short-term pleasures would be a disaster! Our mind could be wandering with anger, negativity, gloomy memories as well as future worries. It is our unfortunate nature to be so.

As such, let's make the most of each day. Schedule it in detail, and reserve some decent time for your own passion.

Indulge in it. Have fun with it! And smile with the meaning that it gives you.

Excite your life the way you wish it could have been!

THE DAY YOU FIND OUT YOUR TRUE SELF

The day you find out your passions and purposes of life is the most important day. It's the day you find out the true inspiration and aspiration of living this life. It's the day you find out the true meaning and excitement of your existence.

It's the day you are reborn.

WAKE UP!

Waste no more days in stress, and get to the life in dreams!

- A life with alluring colors,

With Rapture and Delight,

With Fire and Excitement!

- A Life That You'd NEVER REGRET!

2

REDEFINE NEGATIVITY

The greatest weapon against stress is our ability to choose one thought over another.

- William James

There are only two ways to live your life. One is as though nothing is a miracle. The other is as though everything is a miracle.

- Albert Einstein

It isn't what you have, or who you are, or where you are, or what you are doing that makes you happy or unhappy. It is what you think about.

- Dale Carnegie

For many years, I thought there's nothing worth living for a life confined to the wheelchair,

Until I knew about **Stephan Hawking**.

And I once thought that life has no meaning without arms and legs,

Until I saw **Nick Vujicic** speaking.

Those extreme and unbelievable stories made me wonder, at last, how could people encountering such unfortunate tragedies overcome all disasters and enjoy the days?

How could they move forward and lead a meaningful life?

And how could they make the most of those situations?

On the other hand, it's difficult to see why some famous and wealthy people fell down with life, and ultimately committed suicide without suffering the worst. It's difficult to see how some people can transform tragedies into something empowering, while many others indeed give up and die out at the gate of ordinary obstacles.

The ultimate answer may, in fact, lie inside the mind of the beholder. Different people could look at a specific event from different angles. They could experience the same life yet feel it differently. For some, their minds are shaped to take life seriously and get obsessed with its negative aspects. For others, however, their minds are shaped to have fun with life and see the beautiful sides of it.

The truth is, positive people often have encouraging ways to embrace their hardships and adversaries. For them, an obstacle is no more than a great chance to strengthen their own heart. An obstacle is no more than a bolder way to explore a new day. It is no more than an opportunity to live with courage and strength.

To get rid of negativity and reach for a happier life, as such, it's vitally important to consciously train our mind to think like a true warrior. After all, we don't have to follow the flow of our ordinary thinking. We can instead view life and every hardship from a different perspective. We can give life and everything in it a totally different meaning.

- A fearless and positive meaning.

THE MEANING OF EVERYTHING

The truth is, there is no real meaning of anything in this world.

In fact, all meanings - good, bad and ugly ones - are created inside our own skulls.

All meanings are subjective, and all meanings are just imaginary.

Unsurprisingly, different meanings associated with a specific event could be created by different people. Indeed, there are various angles to look at the same day, and there are various ways to evaluate the same distress. Eventually, your mind depends heavily on previous life experiences to explain and assign a meaning to anything that happened.

Your boss yelled loud at you? Obviously you could feel extremely angry and offended. Later on, however, you learned that he'd been in severe grief due to the death of his daughter. The second time when your boss misbehaved, you might take it less personal and sympathize with him. The meaning of his behavior quickly changed as you learnt more about his life and looked at things from a different perspective.

Your car broke down in the middle of nowhere? Obviously you could feel irritated and start mourning. Or you could think that you were still lucky since at least, the car didn't get damaged and explode in fire. After making peace with your own mind, then, you could start repairing the car or finding your way out of the situation. The feeling you got from the event quickly changed as you changed your perspective and assigned a different meaning to what happened.

You're feeling bored with your job? You can always look for another job or learn to appreciate the one you have. "I just go to office to enjoy myself; work automatically happens." - You can adopt this useful mindset of Jitendra Attra, and see how a single change in perspective dramatically improves your life's quality. Alternatively, you may find out how awesome your job is in terms of helping people and serving this world. Feel supremely excited with its importance and be totally proud of yourself. Imagine all those glory, pride and excitement as you take your steps to work each day. Then put more lively sounds and fabulous colors to that imagination to rock your heart to the furthest extreme.

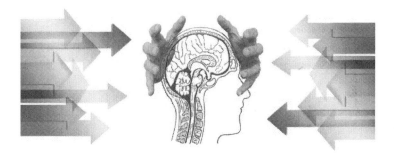

A NEW LIFE IN SIGHT

Enter the inspiring life of Kris Carr.

Kris Carr was initially a dancer, actress and photographer living in New York City. In 2003, however, Kris was diagnosed with a rare stage IV cancer afflicting her liver and lungs. Give up and just wait to die? Not her way! Kris decided to rise up and fight against every odd. She decided to take care of her nutritional lifestyle, knowledge and willpower. Kris wrote about her fighting and experience into a series of New York Times best-selling books. She is now a famous author, a wellness activist and a cancer survivor. Her documentary movie "Crazy Sexy Cancer" was finally released in 2007.

Kris turned her cancer into a business and an inspiration. She turned her cancer into a great opportunity of living and fighting till one's last breath.

Talk about how to make the most of one's situation.

Meet Nick Vujicic.

Nick was born with tetra-amelia syndrome, a rare disorder characterized by the absence of legs and arms.

To see how awful it could have been for him, imagine yourself to be in Nick's situation.

How would you deal with this cruel fate?

How would you go through every day without feeling suffered?

That said, agonizing as his fate is, Nick is currently a famous author and the president of a non-profit organization. He plays, he surfs and he enjoys his life to the utmost. Nick even travels the world and inspires millions of people around. He gives many others motivation to live boldly and to live great. He encourages them to challenge challenges, embrace their life's goodness, and find out the true purposes of their own existence.

Nick is now an outstanding example of making the most of everything available.

The point is, life's quality depends little on what happens to you.

Instead, it is mostly determined by the way you embrace and interpret everything that comes.

After all, your mind creates the meaning of all stress and pains. Your mind creates the meaning of all fear, all rudeness and sorrows. Your mind creates what it means to be good and what it means to be unpleasant.

Eventually, it's not the situation itself that really matters. Instead, it's the story you tell yourself, and the angle from which you look at things that ultimately control your feelings and thus your life's quality. With an appropriate angle on life, as such, you can always cherish and relish this day even if you're going through the most painful situations.

Indeed, it is the story inside your head that really counts.

And it is the story you tell yourself that truly matters.

Fortunately, it is within your control to change what your mind creates, and it is within your power to change the meaning of everything that happens. This is because all meanings are relative: no meaning is fixed, and no meaning is absolutely true.

As such, why don't we discard the meanings that cripple us?

Why don't we choose the meanings that empower our days?

And choose the perspective that spice up our lives more than ever?

Eventually, by changing the perspective from which we view an event, **we can change how we feel** and **how we respond** to it. We can then change our attitude and behaviors towards life and towards others.

The moment you realize this is the moment you can change your whole life. Enormously!

No longer do you have to struggle with all life's ups and downs. No longer do you have to shiver and shatter your dear heart in the darkness of reality. Instead, you can start ruling the quality of your own thoughts and thus your own life. Specifically, you can amplify positive thoughts and reshape negative ones. You can devise a new path for the future, embrace whatever that comes and make the most of it.

Importantly, you should always **be aware** and **question yourself** every time negative feelings arise. **Determine the perspective and the story** you're telling yourself that are causing troubles, and **adjust them appropriately** to pull yourself forward. With that in mind, you can now refine your life's attitude. You can even thank for each pain and sorrow that inflicted you so much in the past. Just let your mind and your thoughts be truly flexible, and your life's quality would never ever be the same.

The moment you realize this is the moment you can control your whole life. Forever!

Hence, for a challenge, start refining what you often tell yourself. Start repeating and embedding these positive confirmations into your mind every day:

"This world is absolutely great. Everyone and everything here is absolutely amazing. And I just need to change my attitude to see that."

"I have immense power to accept everything and forgive everyone that hurt me in life. I can instead smile and gently walk away in knowing that, peace and control always stay with me."

"No matter what happens, I'm really thankful for this amazing and precious life. Why? Because many people still have it worse, much worse than I do! So while trying my best getting out of troubles, I can always feel lucky and grateful for what I do have. And I feel really sorry for many bad fates out there."

"Today, i can take charge and i can conquer everything in life. No one, nothing can ruin my beautiful day. I can make the most of it. I can make the most of this life. And i can make it all truly unforgettable!

I can definitely do that. I can. **I CAN**!"

The secret is, the more you convince yourself and repeat these positive affirmations in mind, the more they will linger on and pull the day forward, and the more glamorous this life will unwind.

Why so? Because after all, we are our dominant thoughts. We are what we think!

So repeat your favorite quotes and positive thoughts every morning. Write them down. Stick them to the wall. Surround yourself with the amazing and inspiring power of positive thinking.

HOW TO MAKE A CHANGE?

How many times you worried ahead, and found the headache to be insignificant?

How many times you imagined the worst, and it all turned out to be a good thing?

And who knows, the trouble at hand will become the best opportunity you'll get. The distress in sight will leave a positive impact on your life.

Who knows?

Enter the story of a farmer and his horse.

One day the horse ran far away. The farmer's neighbors came over and said, "What a bad luck it is!" The farmer replied, "Who knows if it's good or bad? Let's wait and see!"

A few days later, the horse came back and brought several wild horses to the farm. The neighbors celebrated, "Congratulations.

It's so good!" And the farmer replied, "Who knows? Let's see!"

On the very next day, the farmer's son was trying to tame one of the wild horses. He got thrown to the ground with his legs broken. The neighbors came to the farmer, "We're so sorry about your misfortune." The farmer repeated, "Who knows if it's a misfortune or not? Let's see!"

Later that week, the army recruited all healthy young boys in the town to serve in war. The son was not chosen due to his broken legs. The neighbors came over and congratulated. And as usual, the farmer gave the same reply: "Who knows?"

You may recall many times in life that you encountered a series of events like this. In fact, no experience can truly be seen as being good or bad. The distinction between good and bad, lucky and unlucky, fortunate and unfortunate is a very fuzzy one. A "bad" event at this very moment may turn out to be a "good" one later on, and vice versa.

As such, there's no point mourning and complaining about a current situation. Instead, it's always better to make the most of what you do have in hands. It's always better to approach any challenge with courage and optimism in knowing that eventually, it may turn out to be the best turning point in life.

So embrace everything that happens, and just tell yourself, **"Let's see how interesting my life will unfold after this. Let's see!"**

Now, think about an event in life that you're having troubles with, and challenge yourself to see it from a different perspective. Challenge yourself to find the lessons and positive aspects that it can offer.

You can start by asking yourself:

What's good about this?

And how can I take advantage of it?

Maybe it's a chance to shape your courage and deal with anything that comes. Maybe it's a chance to help your Self stronger. Maybe it's a chance to make your God prouder.

And maybe, it's the Life itself conspiring to give you this lesson for a happy and fulfilling life ahead.

Who knows?

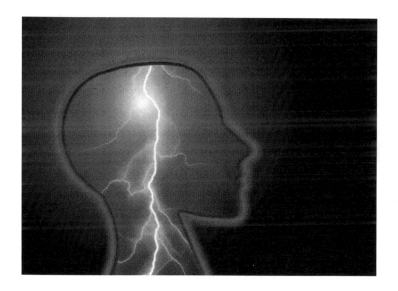

For now, let's learn to reframe an event's meaning towards its positive side.

The rats making noise at night?

Do anything possible to stop that. But if you can't, just think about the good sides. At least you still have a bed to sleep on. At least you know that you're safe there with no dangerous creatures lurking around.

Having no money at all?

Yet at least you're still alive. At least you can give it a try. And at least you can think of some ways to make your life better.

It's just a matter of time.

Being weak at some aspects?

It's great that you are aware of your strengths and weaknesses. With that in mind, you can now devise a plan and make yourself better.

You can start learning new things and growing much more.

Your son is so naughty?

Yet at least you have a child to cherish. At least you have a child that many people wish for.

And at least, you can learn to teach him properly and enjoy seeing him grow up every day.

Your dad yelled loud at you?

Maybe he'd been in severe stress. Maybe he'd been in great troubles. And it's good that he directly told you how he felt.

Coz it could have been worse. Much worse!

Facing a breakup?

Maybe it's a chance for you to find a better person. And it's a chance for you to live a greater life ahead.

It's a chance for you to discover an alternative way in life.

Having a terminal illness?

Still, you can make it an opportunity to be courageous and adventurous. You can write a beautiful song and share your epic fight to the world. You can help revive and inspire millions of people around.

You can make this one the most amazing and meaningful life you've ever wished.

Losing someone you love?

It's truly sad, yet death is never the end of existence. Maybe she'll meet you again in the heaven. Maybe she's enjoying her days in the afterlife. She's wishing that you'll live an upright and meaningful life ahead. And she's hoping that you'll savor every second and every moment of living your day.

And of course you will, won't you?

A DAILY REMINDER

So my friend, whatever happens, you can always rise up and remind yourself that, "At least I still have many things with me".

Whatever happens, you can always smile and remind yourself that, "At least I'm luckier than many others. Coz everything could have been worse, much worse!"

And importantly, spend 10 minutes each day to detect your weak beliefs and thoughts. Then refine them all to lead your life to the right path.

I was lucky to know a dwarf person who was born with a growth hormone deficiency. Judging on the outside, i thought that life would have been really bad for him. I thought that life must have been really sad for him with all troubles and difficulties he had.

Yet it doesn't happen that way! To my amazement, he stays happier and livelier than most people around. How? It's because he views his life as a challenge and testament to his courage. He thanks his life in knowing that, he's still better and luckier than many other lives. In fact, he's still better than many people who are crippling in pain, and he's still better than many others who are dying in vain.

When I was a child, I also thought it'd be too late to start enjoying life if we were already old. That said, I watched the news and learnt that many people started dancing and playing sports at the age of seventy!

I had to think again.

In fact, it's never too late till we stop breathing. It's never too late to start living truly.

It's never too late to start our new life!

♦♦♦

Eventually, being aware of your own beliefs and thoughts, then choosing the ones that truly empower you is the key to success. It is the key to achieving a happy and fulfilling life ahead.

So every day, **remind yourself that you are the ultimate person that's taking control of your own life**. Whatever happens out there, you can always control your inside. You can always control whether you'll die out or you'll rise up. You can always control your attitude towards this life, and what actions you'll take to make the most of it.

Eventually, the art of living great is not about controlling everything in life. Instead, it's about caring and focusing on what you CAN control. Your thoughts included!

Indeed, flexibility and adaptability are the keys of living happily.

Since no road has all roses, and no life is all good.

As such, whatever happens out there, YOU can always to make this life meaningful.

YOU can always make this life great!

3

THE BIGGEST LOVE OF YOUR LIFE

You yourself, as much as anybody in the entire universe, deserve your love and affection.

- Buddha

Love yourself. It's the biggest, sweetest and most romantic love of your life.

- William Than

What lies behind us and what lies before us are tiny matters compared to what lies within us.

- Ralph Waldo Emerson

Life sometimes can get much worse than what you wish it to be.

You may get crippled.

You may be hurt.

You may have fears.

And you may feel lost.

But is life so bad that it is already a dead end?

Absolutely not.

No matter how abysmal and gloomy your day is, you can always find out its bright sides.

And no matter how dreaded it turns out to be, happiness is never unconquerable.

REALIZE YOUR TRUE WORTH

To find your way out of darkness, you must cherish your value. To kill and defeat all distress, you must get to know your own pride.

Recall how kind and amazing you were when you helped people in need? Recall how much you have tried and worked hard in life? Recall how much you've been through and still have survived it all?

Indeed, you yourself have great value, and you yourself have great worth. Importantly, your true value is not up to anyone to decide or judge. It's only up to you!

It's up to how you respect yourself.

Ultimately, you yourself measure your own worth. You yourself realize and decide how great it is!

So embrace your own self.

Embrace your strengths and goodness. Embrace your weaknesses and imperfections.

And cherish your own life. Find out its greatness, its sweetness and its ultimate meaning.

Crucially, feel proud about your own worth without needing anyone to understand or accept it. Because after all, most people are busy struggling with their own lives! As such, they may not view you from an objective perspective, or have enough time to realize your true worth. They may not understand how great a fight you've put up, and how great a person you've been in life.

After all, there is one and only one person that can realize your true worth. There is one and only one person that can truly see how great you are.

It's you. ONLY YOU!

Hence, to overcome every hardship in life, you've got to believe in your own worth.

You've got to believe in your own self!

No matter what happens, you can choose to focus on your very soul. You can choose to close your eyes and feel that inner power released. Feel your power to deal with anyone and anything! Feel your power to conquer any insult, any fear, any loss, any failure.

And in the end, it doesn't matter what the world throws at you. It doesn't matter what happens out there. It doesn't matter at all!

Ultimately, what matters most is that you're staying alive, standing right here on this extraordinary planet, at this exact moment in the cosmic history.

You are still your Self.

You are still your Soul!

ADORE YOUR BEAUTIFUL SOUL

So trust your own self. Trust your own soul. And worship it!

Whenever a trouble comes, just close your eyes and clear your mind. Find your inner peace first.

And breathe deeply.

….

Feel your own breath.

Feel your great Soul.

Let it protect you against all storms and fire. Let it grant you courage to smile in the dark. Let it bring joy and love to your beating veins.

Let it give you strength and goodness to cherish this very existence.

And look into the mirror. Look into your eyes.

Were you too obsessed with daily stress and hassles, and forgot to take care of that person?

Were you too busy with all money and worries, and forgot to feel that soul?

And feel sorry. Feel sorry for ignoring it. Feel sorry for chasing superficial and ephemeral things outside.

Just look at that person. Just look at his eyes. Just look at his smile.

See how wonderful and amazing he is?

In fact, he's the one you should take care and cherish the most. He's the one you should feel proud and fall in love with!

Forever in this life.

REFINE YOUR IDENTITY

Eventually, the way you see yourself determines the quality of your life. It influences how you enjoy the day, and dictates the way you treat other people.

The way you see yourself determines how you accept and defeat the mishaps of life. It influences how you rise up from the abyss, and dictates the way you bounce back from those dark days.

It is extremely important, therefore, to fine tune your self-image and adjust your attitude. Start by learning to realize your value, cherish your worth, and boost your confidence.

Lay out a greater image of yourself, and decide that you'll become it. Decide that you'll act, you'll talk and you'll walk like a new person. Decide that you'll learn, you'll live and you'll love like having a new life.

You're a magical being on a phenomenal planet. You're granted with incredible senses to see, to taste and to feel the world.

You're given a unique chance to adore and explore this beautiful universe.

You're a fearless knight daring your way to be even rougher and tougher.

Nothing, no one can defeat you. No storm, no terror can vanquish you. You are unyielding. You are solid.

And you are unbeatable!

Imagine yourself as the kindest person you've ever known. No matter what happens, you can send warmth and kindness to people. No matter what happens, you can cherish the goodness of everything.

You can treat everyone with care and with love. You can live and you can give. You can forgive and you can forget.

Imagine yourself as the happiest person alive. No matter how this life unfolds, you can keep your heart and your soul intact. You can grow and glow from defeats. You can get stronger and tougher from failures.

You'll cherish this special chance to breathe and exist. You'll reach out for new thrills and experiences. You'll live each day with burning zeal and exhilaration.

You'll live each day as if it were the very last!

RELEASE THE EXCITEMENT WITHIN

What do you need to be happy?

And what do you need to feel excited?

In fact, you'll feel awesome when you get something you need. Maybe when you pass a test or when you win the lottery. The trigger is pulled and you're delighted. You jump up high, you're bright with liveliness.

And you may wonder where that energy comes from.

The energy itself, in fact, comes from your own body and mind. It comes from deep within you!

Indeed, it was just hiding inside, and just waiting for an outside trigger.

That said, why should you need an outside trigger?

While ultimately, you can just become the trigger yourself!

In fact, you can now release that energy from within.

You can now feel ecstatic of being alive.

And be delighted with whatever you've got.

Recall the darkest fates out there, and enjoy your presence.

Recall the darkest times in life, and cherish this present.

Recall the obstacles conquered, feel your own worth, and savor that sweet pride from within.

Indeed, all energy and positivity you need are already inside. They're already within your heart!

And all you need is just to let them out.

You have everything you need. You have every courage and liveliness to relish this life. Maybe you didn't realize that. But you can let them help you, NOW.

It's your call!

You can fall in love with someone special. You can fall in love with yourself. Right now!

You can take control of today's path. You can touch your deepest soul inside, and cherish this very existence.

This ONLY existence!

What's more, it's helpful to redefine what it means to be truly successful. As often, negativity comes from the fact that we feel discontent about our lives and get obsessed with what we can't have. We usually ignore those positive things in life that we are truly blessed, and feel pressured to reach for financial, marital and other successes posed by our societal standards.

Fortunately, this understanding of the very root of our lives' discontentment suggests a pivotal solution: that it's critical to appreciate and enjoy every little thing we have, then challenge our social norms and redefine what it means to be truly successful.

"That man is the richest whose pleasures are the cheapest" – **Henry David Thoreau**

Indeed, we don't need to be rich, to have a beautiful body or get a romantic relationship to be successful in life. We only need to smile often and breathe this fresh air. We only need to savor each frugal meal and appreciate each passing day we have. We only need to be kind and helpful to others. We only need to find out our passions, purposes of existence and take a step towards our greatest dreams.

In fact, we've always been successful in life! We've always possessed various things that many others wish for. And no matter how bad it has been, acknowledge that there are always people out there who do admire us for something we achieved that they couldn't. Years ago, I was stressed out in the middle of my life crisis, and it seemed at first extremely hard to eliminate the stress and negative feelings associated. Until one day, my friend proudly introduced me to his cousin. Not to be expected, this single event made me ponder and altered the very course of my life, forever! Maybe after all, this life was not as dismal as I'd thought, and there were various aspects that I could take notice and indeed felt proud about.

As such, it's extremely crucial to find out your true worth, love all what you have and feel proud about your own Self! Talk to people who are blind, who are crippled or facing a terminal illness, and ask them what it means to be successful. Chances are, your life would never ever be the same!

"To laugh often and love much;

To win the respect of intelligent people and the affection of children;

To appreciate beauty; to find the best in others;

To have played and laughed with enthusiasm and sung with exultation;

To know even one life has breathed easier because you have lived

- This is to have succeeded."

- Ralph Waldo Emerson

THE BIGGEST LOVE IN LIFE

Loving yourself is the key to a beautiful and wonderful life ahead.

You may succeed. You may achieve a lot. But if you always look outside for more and more, you'll be lost. If you forget your inner side and ignore your inner life, you'll be shallow. What's the point of working hard and achieving much, then? What's the point of living this life without even feeling this soul?

You may get bad luck. You may not have much in life. But if you cherish this life, excite your heart, and love yourself, will this day unwind sweet and amazing?

As such, just let yourself be imperfect, be relentless, and be unbeatable!

And be happy. Be excited! Don't wait till you're beautiful. Don't wait till you get rich. Don't wait till you succeed! Coz no one, nothing can make you feel complete. And no richness, no achievement can make you feel fulfilled.

Only you can decide how much is enough. ***Only YOU can!***

You absolutely don't need anyone, and you absolutely don't need anything in this life to feel worthy. After all, people and objects only add more spice and variety to your own life. They're just satellites orbiting around your own world. Therefore, they're not critical to decide your own worth, and they're not crucial to judge your value.

So don't let people decide how you feel and who you are.

And don't let the key of happiness into the hands of others.

Instead, let that key to be you, and only you.

The crucial thing is you. JUST YOU!

After all, your soul is your most important relationship, and it is your most valuable possession.

As always, it feels great if you can get the one or the thing you like. But if you can't, your life can still be amazing and fantastic. Just remember, people and objects only add more spice and variety to your own life. They're not your heart and they're not your soul. They're not your true life.

And they're not who you are in this world!

After all, you yourself are special enough.

You yourself are precious enough.

And you yourself are resilient enough!

As such, why do you need to rely on anything?

And why do you need to rely on anyone?

Ultimately, you don't need anything to be happy.

And you don't need anything to feel excited.

You just need to be YOU!

You just need to love yourself.

And you just need to love your soul.

Love it. Now!

Yell out with power. Jump high with excitement!

Ignite your life, and revive your passion!

Control your smile. Don't wait for anyone. Don't wait for anything to come. Just smile. Just live!

Just love your Self,

And just love your Life

With all your Heart!

Right now, close your eyes.

And taste the pride from within.

Taste the delight from your heart.

Feel. Love. Smile and fly high!

Live!

No matter what happens out there, live!

Truly live!

Just be yourself.

Your Self!

4

COME! I DARE ALL! : THE SUPERB ART OF CRUSHING SUFFERING

The real man smiles in trouble, gathers strength from distress, and grows brave by reflection.

– Thomas Paine

Success is not final, failure is not fatal: it is the courage to continue that counts.

— Winston S. Churchill

Brave men rejoice in adversity, just as brave soldiers triumph in war.

- Lucius Annaeus Seneca

Most superheroes you know probably endured something traumatic in life.

Bruce Wayne witnessed his father and mother murdered in front of him. He got tormented with mere pain and distress throughout childhood. He got obsessed with finding out the reason and the person behind his parents' death.

Barry Allen's mother was killed by a speedster. His father was wrongly accused of her death and was put into prison. Later in life, Barry also encountered a dramatic accident that transformed his life forever.

Oliver Queen was desperate after the sink of the Queen's Gambit. In the life raft, Oliver witnessed his father shooting himself just to save others. He subsequently experienced innumerable dangers and sufferings for years living on the island.

All superheroes you know probably endured times and times again surrounded by darkness.

Painful and tragic,

Tricky and bitter,

Hellish as miseries are, it is the endurance of all those agonies that shaped their courage. It is the comeback from those dark days that made them heroes. It is the resilience they developed that defined who they were. If not for those painfully dark days, would they still have been Batman, Spider Man, The Flash or The Arrow? You could probably doubt that.

CONFRONT IT ALL

We all have dark days,

With ill fate and regrets,

Wish distress and headaches,

With dismay and sadness.

The problem is, sometimes we are not bold enough to accept the challenge. We are not brave enough to stare in its face. We are not resilient enough to fight hard, or bounce back. And we are not sapient enough to recognize our own strength.

In fact, the more we fear challenges, the less peace and freedom we'll get.

The more we let problems in charge, the less wisdom and growth we'll gain.

And paradoxically, the more we confront all dangers and distresses, the better we can control destiny.

The more we accept misery, and even challenge more of it to come, the sweeter our life will unwind.

Because ultimately, if we're scared and run away from something, it will chase after and haunt us.

But if we confront and run towards that thing, it will let go and keep us in peace.

The more we fight with life, the more we'll lose. The more we embrace it all, the more we'll win.

That's how life works!

THE SWEETNESS OF PRIDE

The lesson learnt is that, therefore, we can approach any difficult feeling and situation in life in a bolder way.

We can embrace instead of evading.

We can defy instead of denying.

And we can hold dear instead of fearing.

Why? Because ultimately, bravery is the origin of something extraordinary and exceptional: the sweetness of victory, of getting proud

- **The sweetness of our own pride.**

Indeed, the tougher life turns out, the greater chance you can get,

To let the world know who you are, and how strong you can be;

To stand out above the crowd;

To prove that you are in no way ordinary!

And that you are able to deal with life extraordinarily.

Bitter life, better you!

Cruel fate, prouder you.

So let pride be the killer of pains.

And let being proud be your antidote of sorrows.

THANK YOU, CHALLENGES!

Hence, let's stop fleeing away from obstacles. Let's start facing all with courage and confidence, and even challenging more to come.

So that we can defeat test after test, challenge after challenge!

So that we can nurture the sweetness of victories, rejoice the pride inside our hearts, and let the world know how strong we can be.

Like life's true heroes.

Let's thank hardships for giving us a great chance to learn, to grow and harden.

Thank hardships for giving us an opportunity to review our lives' goals and purposes.

And perhaps, a superhero may arise from those dark days - A superhero of our own self - A superhero with courage, kindness, and resilience

- A superhero from within.

Recall your darkest days, and see how brave you've come?

Recall your difficult times, and see how sublimely you've fought?

Recall all the fears, all the tears, all the pains and sorrows you've had. See how great it is that you did survive everything and make it this far?

As such, let's be bolder. Let's be tougher!

Be imperfect. Be relentless. And be unstoppable!

Let courage and pride guide your own path. Let the flame of heart incinerate any ache that comes!

And don't wish for a smooth life. Wish that life will be tough, really tough, and that you are tougher than it all!

PRACTICE MAKES PERFECT

What doesn't kill you can make you stronger. Yet just don't let hardships kill you before you can get real strong. To eliminate negativity and disasters in life, therefore, it is critical to build and nurture your courage every moment. It is important to shape and practice resilience every day.

Ultimately, the secret of crushing suffering lies inside your own heart. **In fact, using strong and positive emotions to dominate and incinerate a negative one** is a marvelous method that can help eliminate negativity in life. And among all positive emotions that human possess, the sweetness of getting proud stands out as one of the most fabulous and powerful weapons.

As such, it's now time to challenge every ordinary obstacle that you previously avoided. Whenever a problem comes up, you can tell yourself:

"I love this test despite its bitterness. And I even want more of it to come!

This test is, indeed, a great chance to act like a true hero, a great chance to show this world who I am today!

And it is exactly what I want to experience.

I embrace it all.

And I dare it all!"

So turn every pain into a chance of being great. Turn every headache into a chance of living strong. Truly strong!

And make your tears into something sweet. Make your risk into something entertaining. Make your breathing soul proud of your heart.

Nurture your courage, and get well prepared! So that you can gently smile when real tests arrive. So that you can revive happiness even when the darkness of reality slaps straight in the face.

And during hard times, let's read encouraging books and watch inspiring movies about the courage of people. Let's see how they could challenge challenges and turn danger into opportunity. Let's see how they could survive and thrive despite any mishap that comes.

Let's see what made them true heroes.

Enter the courage of Bethany Hamilton.

Hamilton developed a love for surfing early in childhood. One day in 2003, unfortunately, she encountered a traumatic shark attack on the Tunnels Beach of Kauai. She survived the dramatic struggle with her left arm bitten off.

What should she do about this unfortunate reality? Complain about her life and just give up?

Not her way! Hamilton was extremely determined and returned to her surfboard merely one month later, and ultimately became victorious in professional surfing. She won the first place in the Explorer Women's Division of the NSSA National Championships. And she wrote about her extreme battle in her autobiography "Soul Surfer: a true story of faith, family, and fighting to get back on the board". In 2011, the movie "Soul Surfer" was released.

Talk about courage and determination!

Meet Aron Ralston.

Ralston was stuck in Utah's Blue John Canyon in 2003 when a boulder dislodged and trapped his hand in place. He had to struggle with dehydration and hypothermia for almost six days. With no hope of getting rescue in sight, he made a brave decision to amputate his right forearm using a pocketknife. He crawled out of the place and got rescued several days after.

Ralston is admired for making a brave and difficult decision that most people couldn't have. His story is now made into the movie "127 hours" which inspires and encourages millions of lives around the world.

Ralston is a great example of fighting and surviving against extreme odds.

Right now, with this courageous mindset inside, let's identify a major problem that you've been avoiding. Have a decent plan to deal with it, and face it head-on today.

Close your eyes. Feel your own breath. And forget everything outside.

Recall the difficult life that you have passed. Recall how great it is that you could give it a fight and survive everything?

Now, let that sweetness of pride surge inside your beating heart. Let that exhilaration permeate and penetrate every corner of your soul.

Let it devour every hardship and every darkness that comes by. Let it annihilate every ache and bitterness that's rioting from within.

Close your eyes, and feel your excitement as this opportunity comes close. The trouble in sight will be a chance to become great. The distress coming will be a chance to cherish your soul, to feel the eagerness, sweetness and enthusiasm of its pride.

And imagine yourself, with the greatest confidence in the world, staring at the challenge, pointing straight at its face, and yelling out loud: **"Come, I want you. And I dare you!"**

Feeling difficult with your job? Want more weekends and hate all Mondays? "Come! I love the challenges at work, i love solving them all! I'll await and long for Monday. I'll show my courage and skills, and I'll be proud of myself!"

Feeling disturbed by people? "Come! I love dealing with difficult people. I feel proud to learn more. I'll await and long for any encounter, and I'll challenge everything that comes!"

Having fear or hesitation? "Come! I love taking this challenge, and i'll be proud of this Self. I'll act, I'll talk, I'll walk like a true hero. And I'll show this world who I am today!"

Feeling pained, lost, worried, lonely, depressed? "No more! Now i can challenge everything in life! I know that this feeling is just temporary. I know that it's just testing my courage. I am proud of myself, and I am willing to embrace it all. Come!"

The sooner you release your inner courage and strength, the sooner you'll find this Life fantastic.

The sooner you relish every day and everything that comes, the sooner you'll find this YOU amazing!

Be brave!

Be proud of your heart.

Be in love with your soul.

Be the superhero that you like.

Be the superhero of your life!

Cancer?

Death?

Loss?

Fear?

Stress?

Regret?

Worry?

Agony?

And Catastrophe?

COME! I DARE ALL!

5

YOUR INNER SAVIOR

We are more often frightened than hurt, and we suffer more from imagination than from reality.

- Lucius Annaeus Seneca

Imagination is more important than knowledge. Knowledge is limited. Imagination encircles the world.

- Albert Einstein

Imagination is the only weapon in the war against reality.

- Lewis Carrol

Our human machine is an astonishing and complicated system, with its various organs and tissues fitting together into one united body.

Yet that machine is far from being perfect.

As a matter of fact, our mind often has difficulty distinguishing actual memories from a vivid imagination. And our emotion can be affected simply by imagining a positive event like love, fun, success, or by imagining negative ones like fear, stress and worry.

Vivid imagination can alter our perception of reality to the utmost.

As such, why don't we delete negative imagination to eradicate daily sadness?

And why don't we develop positive ones to bring hope and excitement to our life?

In fact, vivid imagination can be applied to alter our inner perception, especially when it comes to a painful or monotonous time. It can indeed turn into a great savior during our own hardships.

Meet Vera Fryling.

Vera was a little child living under cover in Berlin during the traumatic World War 2 Holocaust. During her darkest time, she imagined herself to be a doctor living freely and enjoying every day of it. And the result? She defeated every hardship, every disease and danger along the way. She remarkably made the most of her situation and imagination.

In her own words: "Imagination can help one transcend the insults life has dealt us".

Enter the struggle of Colonel George Hall of the U.S Air Force.

Hall was imprisoned for seven years after being captured in the Vietnam War. Every day living in prison, nevertheless, he closed his eyes and imagined himself to be playing an interesting game of golf! His vivid imagination altered his reality to the very point that he could survive those difficult days and even relish his own existence.

His masterful skill of imagination saved his very soul and let him make the most of every day in life. Even in prisons!

Or talk about top athletes.

Most of them usually visualize themselves being in the real contest just minutes before it started. They vividly imagine every block, every step and movement along the way. They even clearly feel the extreme heat and endurance of the race in mind.

They put themselves into a competent state just before it actually happens to get the best result.

The ultimate secret is that we can act as if the imagination were real and already achieved. Rather than thinking it as something that's coming from the far future, imagine it as something that you're genuinely experiencing right now, at this exact moment in time. The more detailed and vivid that imagination becomes, the more dramatic it can alter our emotion and perception of reality. And with that in hand, our quality of life would never ever be the same.

Coz after all, we are what we believe.

In fact, many times in life, we don't have much power to control whatever accidents that happen, and we don't have much power to control whatever the environment will become. Indeed, some people will get good luck and some others will get bad one. That's how life works! That's what we have to understand and eventually accept.

That said, whatever happens, we can always control the

inside environment. We can always control what we think. We can always control what we feel.

And we can always control what we imagine!

During hard times, let your imagination fly far to the deepest world. Let it revive your own heart. Let it be your dearest friend, and give you the greatest joy of living this life. After all, no chain and shackle can detain it. No pain and prison can limit it!

So enjoy the sweetness that your wildest imagination serves you. It's always here with you, and for you!

1. MAKE PEACE WITH DESIRES

Having headaches with cravings and desires?

Just close your eyes, and imagine. Imagine that you're right there on the road towards your dream. Can you imagine how wonderful it is that you can plan and step towards it?

Imagine that you can obtain the thing you love. Really soon! Imagine that you're absolutely comfortable working towards it, and that you're absolutely patient waiting for it.

After all, there's no need to rush, there's no need to worry, and there's no need to desire so much.

Coz you have the power to succeed with life. And you have the power to accomplish your sweetest dream.

Coz with hard work and determination, it's in your hand!

2. CONQUER ALL WORRIES

Stress and worries can make you look bad, so why waste your

time wrestling with them at all?

Let's just relax, and breathe deeply.

Imagine the coming events as necessary lessons for you to learn. Imagine that they would ultimately serve a good purpose. And imagine how those challenges would make you much stronger.

Imagine how proud you'd be to boldly face it all!

Relax, and just close your eyes. Imagine the worst that could happen to you.

How bad could it be?

Realize that you're not going to jail, and that you're not going to suffer an agonizing death. Realize that it's not the end of the world! Even if you're going to die, it's not the worst death and pain ever! Many people still suffer it worse. Much worse! Yet many can find their inner peace and joyfulness. Many can find the courage to smile and fight against it all.

Imagine, and get used to the worst that could happen to you. It's not a big deal!

It's not the worst in the world.

And it's not the end!

Imagine it. Contemplate it.

Learn to face it, and learn to deal with it today. Bravely!

Relax, and open your eyes. Congratulations! You've nicely dealt with the worst that could happen to you.

So let's cheer up! Since things could never get worst!

And from now on, everything could only get better. From now on, this very life could only get better!

3. ERASE YOUR PAST

Whatever happened yesterday, there is no need to let it linger.

Imagine.

No matter how bad it has been, imagine it's the exact lesson that you need to learn.

It's the exact opportunity that you need to grow.

It's the exact road towards your dreams.

And it's the exact life experience that you wish for.

Do you want to have a great life?

Then simply, don't wish for a life that you can't have. But wish for the very life that you do own, and wish that you know how to make the most of everything available.

After all, there is no need to regret, and there is no need to obsess your mind with the long gone past.

The past cannot be changed. The past is just over. And the past cannot hurt you anymore.

Unless you let it to!

Today is a new day, and today is a new chapter.

So let's start a new life!

Just let the past be in the past.

And let bygones be bygones!

4. ADORE THE PRESENT

Let your imagination go wild and fly real far.

Imagine now.

Imagine how great it would be to be walking around and seeing the world. Now let your soul fly far to remote stars and distant planets. And let yourself be supremely excited while riding elephants and meeting dinosaurs.

Imagine how great it would be that you could perceive and experience new things. Imagine how great it'd be if you could climb mountains and travel the past. Imagine all the delight and excitement of the bumpy road ahead.

Imagine how far and exhilarating it'd be if your mind could fly to the bluest sky, and smile with this beautiful world.

Right now, just close your eyes.

Feel your body and soul.

Imagine that you just met a tragic accident. Imagine that you just lost your own hands or your own eyes. Imagine that you just lost your own life.

Relax….

And open your eyes.

Feel so lucky for being right here, right now.

Feel so lucky for this breathing, smiling, for this feeling of being alive.

And for everything that you've got.

Eventually, there is no need to complain, and there is no need to blame so much. Since no matter how bad life's been for you, many people still have it worse. Much worse!

You're lucky. I'm lucky. We're all lucky. Coz no matter what happened, life could have been worse. Much worse!

Be glad with what you do own, until you can get what you love most.

Be excited with this very life, and savor every second of it!

5. AWAIT THE FUTURE

Await the future. The best time is still ahead.

Close your eyes, and imagine.

Imagine that your gloomy days will pass. Imagine that brighter days will come. Really soon!

Imagine that you'll never give up your dreams. You'll move on and always hope for the best. Always!

Imagine. Imagine that you'll scream out loud and crush any sorrow, and that you'll hold your bold fist to defeat anything.

Anything!

Coz ultimately, everything is just fleeting. Every hardship is just temporary.

And you won't know how great it is at the end of the road.

Until you decide to move on!

6. BE YOUR BEST SELF

Imagine being your best self today.

Imagine that your future self is looking back at you.

And find something special that you can do right now. Imagine how you can make this very second great, and how you can make this very moment count.

Imagine you're a true hero today.

Imagine how strong and resilient you can get. Imagine how great and brave you can be. Imagine how splendid a fight you can have.

No matter what comes!

Feel your strength. Feel your confidence. And feel your elation from within.

Walk like your best self. Talk like your best self. And act like your best self.

Just be your best self. Today!

7. REVIVE YOUR DREAMS

Erase your bad habits.

Think about one bad habit that you possess.

And imagine how damaging it can inflict upon you.

How painful will it hurt your loved ones and others?

And how REGRETFUL will you get at the end of this life?

Beat your procrastination.

Think about the life in your dream, and what you'll need to do to reach it.

Imagine:

How regretful will you be if you hesitate, and how painful will you get if you just give up?

If you don't start taking action now, how much ache will you have?

And if you start doing it now, how much triumph will you win?

Imagine the feeling of success.

Imagine the extreme excitement as you live the life you wish.

Imagine how sweet it'll be as you reach to your dreams.

Imagine how impressive it'll get when you turn into your best,

And how proud you'll be if you can beat any pain.

Defeat your fear and procrastination. Defeat your laziness and lousy habits. And start working towards your ultimate dreams.

Come on! You CAN make it!

6

WHERE TO FIND THE RESILIENCE YOU NEED?

Whenever you find yourself doubting how far you can go, just remember how far you have come. Remember everything you have faced, all the battles you have won, and all the fears you have overcome.

Then raise your head high and forge on ahead, knowing that YOU GOT THIS!

– Anonymous

Before success comes in any man's life, he's sure to meet with much temporary defeat and, perhaps some failures. When defeat overtakes a man, the easiest and the most logical thing to do is to quit. That's exactly what the majority of men do.

- Napoleon Hill

Out of massive suffering emerged the strongest souls; the most massive characters are seared with scars.

- Khalil Gibran

Close my eyes and i feel my mind. At this exact moment in time, trillions of neuronal connections and chitchatting are creating the very thoughts of my brain.

What a great feeling.

Our human brain is indeed an amazing and complicated system, and among the most impressive feats that it can perform, adaptability is one of great help. Our adaptability allows us to bounce back and thrive despite many life's odds. It can help us stabilize and adapt to every downfall.

No matter what really happened.

The mind's adaptability can also help us habituate to our old feelings, and give us immense passion to discover novel things in life. In fact, we tend to seek for new fun and pleasures. We tend to get excited with new bliss and experiences.

Importantly, we can take advantage of this curiosity. We can acquire more fervor by trying new hobbies and enjoying new leisure. We can also use it to learn new skills and knowledge each day.

We can be creative and imaginative!

THE ACHE OF CRAVING

On the other hand, be aware of the negativity of your longing if you let it go far. At times you could desire so much for new fun and experiences. You could be tormented by the ache of craving, and get obsessed with the very life that you can't have.

As such, it's important to remind yourself to value everything that you're granted, and remind yourself to make the most of every fun available.

Remind yourself of what you do have. And feel sorry for people that don't!

Remind yourself that the desire is just fleeting, and that the craving is just temporary. You'll find it unimportant shortly, and you'll find it unnecessary shortly!

Remind yourself to wait for some time before making a decision, and wait for some days before purchasing a new thing. This invaluable buffer would give your mind a chance to habituate to the desire. This precious time would help your Self crave less and evaluate more. This way, you'll make fewer mistakes and have less regrets in life.

EVERY PAIN WILL END

Crucially, the adaptive mechanism of our brain helps us habituate to our negative feelings. Our minds can adjust, adapt and eventually control negativity over time.

Enter the resilience of Frederick Douglass.

Mr. Douglass was born into slavery in Talbot County, Maryland in 1818. He had to endure the extreme violence of his time and was separated from his parents early in life. Against all odds, however, Douglass escaped slavery at the age of twenty and turned into a prominent American abolitionist. He fought real hard for the human rights and became one of the most eminent intellectuals of the 19th century.

His will to persist and defeat all difficulties was a prime example of fighting for one's life and freedom. It exemplifies the extreme bravery and resilience of the human will.

Meet Stephan Hawking.

Mr. Stephan was enjoying his life in university until one day, a rare form of motor neuron disease struck him. Gradually, he got paralyzed over the coming decades. He spent the rest of his life in the wheelchair and could only communicate via a robotic device. His bright future seemingly fragmented into mishap and agony.

How could he cope with such a tragedy?

How could he accept everything and stride forward?

He couldn't, at first. He almost crumbled under the ache of his fate, and almost collapsed from the agony of reality. But no pain is forever, and no loss is everlasting. Stephan gradually rose up and fought for his own life. He accepted his fate and strived to make the most of it. And today, the world knows about Stephan Hawking as a top physicist, a prolific writer, and an inspiring example of thriving against all odds.

His encouraging story has been a great motivation for many others, and is nicely made into the movie "The theory of everything".

Are you finding the resilience you need?

- Just recall your difficult days.

Recall how many times you wrestled with a headache, and finally found it to be unimportant?

How many times you feared to climb the mountain ahead, and finally found it to be so easy?

How many times you lived your days in worry, and finally found it to be insignificant?

Truth to be told, we could be engulfed by negative feelings at various points throughout life. During difficult days, we tend to think that it's the end of the world. We tend to think that it's a blind alley with all miseries and distress ahead. Yet somehow we can conquer them all. Somehow we can get the courage and strength to move forward. Somehow we can survive every pain and push everything into oblivion.

In fact, we tend to exaggerate the distress in sight.

We tend to inflate the hassle ahead.

We underestimate how brave and stable our body is.

And we underestimate how wise and versatile our mind can be.

Fear and stress, regret and worry, anxiety and distress, each and every feeling will pass. Every bad day will fade. Every ache will depart.

Given that you allow it to leave!

That being said, sometimes it could be extremely hard to eliminate a negative feeling inside. Just recognize that it's absolutely normal for a negative feeling to dominate, and all you have to do is simply **get busy** and **focus your attention elsewhere**, in knowing that time will soon do its magic and bring you back to balance. You can simply make new friends and talk with them via social apps like Bigo Live or Meetup. You can play with your pets, read an inspiring book, watch a good movie, play your favorite games, watch the news, take a walk, sing out loud, recall encouraging quotes, focus on others' pains and courage, improve your needed skills or finish your current work. Just ignore the troubles in sight and temporarily get away from it in knowing that eventually, you'll feel much better.

And to free your life from headaches, always keep in mind **Carlson's rules: don't sweat the small stuff, and it's all small stuff!**

Ultimately, we're all just tiny particles living on a miniscule planet, floating endlessly in this immense universe. Everything and everyone we meet is just a transitory phenomenon. Even this pain, this worry, this regret or sorrow, even this life and even this world, everything is merely a fleeting existence in the extraordinary cosmic timeline. Everything, everyone we know will all one day turn into dust and oblivion. They all will sooner or later vanish and die out. No one, nothing can escape that eventual fate. As such, don't let yourself stuck with yesterday's pains or tomorrow's troubles. Smile on and move on with courage, and see how this endless time erases every ache you have.

Hence, my friend, if you're having troubles and heartaches in life, remind yourself that your pains and sorrows are just temporary. They will soon vanish into the past, and they will soon dwindle into oblivion!

It's just a matter of time.

Remind yourself that soon they can no longer bug you. Soon they will be nothing much!

Remind yourself that tomorrow, life will get better. And tomorrow will be a finer day.

Remind yourself that your body and mind will soon adapt to the matter at hand; That you yourself have the plan and courage to conquer it.

Hence, don't wish for a placid life. Embrace the headaches that you do have, and wish that you'll find the resilience to beat it all.

In fact, you have immense resilience and courage buried deep within.

You have everything you need to defeat all difficulties.

You have everything you need to defeat all agonies and mishaps.

You just need to tap into that power.

You just need to be your true self!

So ignore your feelings.

Ignore all distractions and disturbances.

Now just step forward.

And do whatever you need to.

Believe in your own courage.

Believe in your own wisdom.

And have faith in your life's path.

Have faith in yourself.

Your Self!

7

NOT YOURS, IT'S MY FAULT!

We are made wise not by the recollection of our past, but by the responsibility for our future.

- George Bernard Shaw

The greater part of our happiness or misery depends upon our dispositions, and not upon our circumstances.

– Martha Washington

You cannot escape the responsibility of tomorrow by evading it today.

- Abraham Lincoln

Once in a while, bad news falls upon you.

You may blame outside events for making your days suffered.

You may blame your parents. They couldn't give you a perfect setting to thrive and succeed. They didn't understand and accept your way when you needed them most.

You may blame your own boss. He didn't respect you. He scolded when you messed things up, and never complimented when you made things right. He didn't give you the support and encouragement needed.

You may blame your own fate. Maybe you're born with disabilities. Maybe you're born with a bad appearance. Maybe you're born with disasters and accidents that afflicted your fate.

As often, blaming outside events and other people can make us feel better. Our brain can find excuses for any traumatic event and mistake that happened. That way, we can feel good momentarily. That way, we can be justified and we can be right.

In the long run, however, that will lead us to even more troubles and headaches. We can put all blames outside, and we can put all responsibility on others.

But guess what? Rarely can we control the outside, and rarely can we control other people. As such, blaming outside will bring us a life with no control. No control at all!

In reality, blaming everything and everyone around is usually the easiest and most automatic way of our daily reactions. Yet often, we forget the most important factor that decides our life:

Self!

Indeed, it's our own Self that truly matters! It's our Self that can decide the quality of living, and it's our Self that can control the direction of our life's path.

It's sometimes difficult to accept that, indeed. It's difficult to take full responsibility for whatever happens, and it's difficult to take full charge of everything in life. It's difficult, extremely difficult! Yet it is a must if we want to get a better day. And it is a must if we want to reach for a better life.

WHY RESPONSIBILITY?

So why, after all, is taking responsibility for your situation always better? Here are the reasons:

1. Responsibility gives you control of your situation

By taking responsibility for whatever happens, you are no longer passively affected by your environment. You can now stop blaming and complaining about life. You can now change your thoughts to alter your internal feelings, and change your deeds to alter your external outcomes.

2. You can adapt to the situation

By taking full charge of your day, you can now adapt to the way other people behave, and you can now adapt to the way the world operates.

You no longer need your life to be exactly the way you wish it to be!

3. Taking responsibility for everything allows you to grow

By putting responsibility on your own shoulder, you can have a great opportunity to learn from your mistakes. You can have a great chance to grow and flourish. Your annoying colleague teaches you the lesson of skills and communication. Your stubborn kid teaches you the lesson of love and understanding. Your dismal fate teaches you how to find out the bright sides of life, and thrive from it.

This way, responsibility can turn your pain into strength. Responsibility can turn your sorrow into tomorrow's glow.

TAKE CHARGE OF EVERYTHING HAPPENED

Each and every day, there are many unexpected twists and turns that can happen. Maybe it's a bastard that yells loud at you. Maybe it's a rude spouse that breaks your heart. Maybe it's an accident that robs you of your love.

It's not your fault. Not at all!

Yet if you only focus on what you can't do, you'll lose all hope.

And if you solely blame outside events and people, you'll lose all control.

Why?

Because rarely can you change the world like you wish, and rarely can you make others to your way. Eventually, you can only get more control by taking charge of life's ups and downs. You can only get more control by focusing on what you **CAN** do.

After all, you are responsible for what you feel.

Maybe you are responsible for not preparing needed skills to deal with the situation. You are responsible for interpreting the ultimate meaning of all events, and deciding whether they're just small tests or they're in fact impossible to overcome.

You are responsible for deciding what is important and what is not.

Ultimately, you can let mishaps go far and work for a beautiful life ahead, or you can let them forever linger on mind. You can take control of what to keep and what to give. You can decide on what to leave and what to forget.

Ultimately, you can let yourself crumble under the distress of life, or you can put everything behind and move on with it.

It's your choice!

And you are responsible for what you do.

You are responsible for your own response to the mishaps of life. You are responsible for planning and designing your own path, and for whatever you get on and perform after.

Always, the choice is yours. Always yours!

As often, the source of negative feelings comes from the fact that we feel out of control of our external circumstances. We feel powerless in trying to achieve a perfect life that we wish for. Anger, sadness, depression and negativity may ultimately come from this feeling of having no control buried deep within.

In fact, as we try to blame anyone or anything outside, we'll automatically lose our sense of control. And with that, anger, hatred, depression and other negative feelings may arise. This doesn't mean that we should always try to blame ourselves, but instead recognize our part that could have caused the problem in the first place, our part in choosing which angle we use to look at that situation, and how we respond to it.

Eventually, it's critical to eliminate our feeling of hopelessness inside in order to achieve a great life. No matter how awful the world and its people have mistreated you, always **feel your power to control your life's direction.** After all, you **don't need to care so much** about who or what let you down. You just need to take control of your own explanations of all events' meanings, and take charge of what you'll do afterwards. You just need to **be totally confident** and **feel totally proud of your own control.** You just need a brave heart to embrace and face anything in life.

The ultimate secret is to act as if you have immense control over your life's quality. Even if you can't change people and the outside world, you can always change your inside environment to adapt to all outside circumstances. You can always change your perspective from which you look at things. You can always adjust your expectations for the world and its people. You can shift your focus to the positive aspects of everything. You can then just take actions to reach for the life you wish instead of passively waiting for it to come. If you can take responsibility and control over all of these aspects, you are unstoppable! No one, nothing in this world can prevent you from reaching for your own happiness.

As such, remove the thought of being a victim, and let yourself become the hero of your life. Importantly, don't wait for that happy and fulfilling life to come. It rarely does! Instead, you can now take control and create it yourself. Just be courageous. Be relentless. And be unstoppable!

Remember, the art of living great is not about controlling everything in life. Instead, it's about caring and focusing on what you CAN control. Your thoughts and your actions included.

YOU GOT HIT. WHAT SHOULD YOU DO?

So my friend, whenever you encounter something traumatic and difficult to swallow, stop raging and blaming outside. Stop obsessing your mind with negativity first.

And think about people who have worse, much worse situation than yours. Think about people who are in pain yet still succeed.

What makes the difference?

Maybe it's their attitude. Maybe they take full responsibility for their own thoughts. They take full charge of their actions, and they don't dwell so much on the negative experiences in sight.

Maybe they ponder upon the events' positive aspects. They think about what they can learn from the mistakes, and how much strength they can gain from beating those disasters.

Successful people focus on what they CAN do. They focus on HOW to make the most of any situation!

In fact, there're many people out there who have much more terrible and more abominable fates than ours. Much worse than ours! Yet they can still achieve and succeed. They can still be happier than we are.

Meet Oprah Winfrey.

Oprah was unfortunately born in a poor family and was raised in terrible conditions. As a child, Oprah was raped many times and got pregnant when she was only fourteen years old. Her child was soon born in reluctance, but he was severely ill and passed away shortly after.

In Oprah's situation, everyone could easily deem this life as a cruel and hopeless abyss. Most people in her shoes would easily give up and die out in vain. How about Oprah? Did she surrender and perish?

Not at all! Oprah turned her pain into her strength. She believed that she could shape her life into a happy and worthy path. She believed that she could make it all a difference! Step by step, Oprah put all traumatic aches and sufferings in the past, and focused relentlessly on the road toward her dreams.

Eventually, Oprah is now the first American's black billionaire and one of the most powerful women alive. Glorious success and fulfillment are the ultimate rewards for her very decision to take control of her life.

Enter the tragic fate of W Mitchell.

Mitchell was unfortunately involved in a blazing motorcycle accident at the age of just twenty eight. His face and body were severely burnt, and his fingers were almost lost. Against all excruciating ache and agony of his fate, nevertheless, he fought his way out of darkness and came back to life.

Four years later, sadly enough, Mitchell encountered a paralyzing plane crash while going for a business trip. His life was almost lost, his spinal cord was severely injured, and Mitchell was forced to live the rest of his life in a wheelchair.

Tormented and got defeated by this cruel fate? Not his way! Mitchell began to take full charge of his feelings and actions. He gradually learnt to accept and thrive from those dark days. To reach for his life dreams, Mitchell **focused** relentlessly on what he **could** do. He focused solely on the road forward. And that's not all, he even found the woman of his life and got married several years later.

Today, Mitchell is one of the most impossible person alive, and an inspiring example of living without fearing.

The point is, it's not your fate or your situation that matters most.

It's you. Only YOU!

Many times in life, you may not have much control over outside events. You may not have much control over how they will change. But you can always control how you approach them, and whatever you'll do afterwards.

Let's look around us.

Everyone has their own problems and hardships. Many people have to live the darkest walks of life. Many of them have to face the painful call of death. Yet somehow, they can still take charge and then move forward. Somehow, they can still gain strength and happiness from those darkest days.

That's the reason why you can, and why you must take charge of your own thoughts. You must take charge of your own actions as well as everything in life.

Eventually, to defeat every difficulty in sight, you must believe that you can control your own life. You must believe in your own strength.

You must believe in your own self!

After all, you yourself are the biggest factor that decides the quality of life.

You yourself are the biggest master that decides the direction of it.

You yourself are the greatest enemy of living truly!

And you yourself are the biggest obstacle to a great and fulfilling life ahead.

The moment you recognize this is the moment you can grow up and take control. It's the moment you can touch the immense power and capability within.

Hence let's stop blaming, and let's start dealing with everything that comes.

Even if it was others' fault, even if it was an accident that happened unexpectedly, you can always take control. You can always take charge of the day. Don't waste the only life you have for blaming. Don't waste the only life you have for complaining.

The next time you realize that you're making an excuse, try your best to stop it. Immediately!

Then take full control. And just look inside.

Examine your own thoughts and actions, and determine what are going wrong.

What are the weaknesses and negativity in your own thoughts?

What are the weaknesses in your habits that could be improved?

What can you learn from this failure?

How can you take advantage of your situation and make the most of it?

How can you find out its bright sides, and turn it into an opportunity?

You've got cancer?

You may feel pain. You may face death. And you may lose everything in life?

Yet you can take charge of it. You can be a living example of courage and strength. You can write an inspiring book. You can raise a charity fund. You can inspire others to live better, to live bolder, and to be fantastic. You can make it all a difference!

You can make your name forever etched into the heart of everyone.

What a great opportunity it is!

You've lost the love of your life?

Your eyes bleed. Your heart breaks. And your ache agonizes every day?

Yet you can take control and see it differently. Maybe your love is happy living in another world. Maybe she's enjoying it so much there. And she's always watching you from the heaven.

Maybe she's praying that you'll be strong. Maybe she's wishing that you'll live a wonderful life ahead, and she's hoping that you'll savor the richness and greatness of living this life.

Maybe she's waiting for you to make it all unforgettable. And she'll be delighted to hear about your journey and wonderful stories in the afterlife.

Would you make her disappointed, then?

NURTURE YOUR SKILLS

Practice makes perfect. In order to control and take charge of your life, you'll need to practice that every day.

For a start, be aware and take control of your own emotions. It's vitally important to be happy with whatever you do own. Be glad with everyone and everything around first, until you can be with the ones and the things that you love most.

After all, the more we embrace life as it is, the more we'll win. And the more we fight against it, the more we'll lose.

Ultimately, life always wins!

Enter the "Groundhog Day" movie. Phil was a weatherman who was finding himself annoyed with many people and many things in life. Until one day, something mysterious happened as he found himself reliving the same day again and again.

What could he do? Phil gradually learnt to accept the fact and enjoy the day. He began to appreciate everyone and everything in it. He began to get happy, be helpful to others, and take full charge of the day.

Talk about a dramatic change in one's perspective and life quality.

After being aware of your own emotions, you can then learn from other people who overcame the same dilemma.

You can search on Google, you can read books and ask others around. You can learn necessary lessons and skills from them:

How could they stay cool and calm in dealing with difficult people and situations in sight?

How could they smile and enjoy everything in life, even with broken legs and severed arms?

What thoughts and plans did they have?

Excruciating as their hardships were, how could they still find out the meaning of living their lives?

Facing a conflict?

"No problem. No big deal! Many people have to live with even worse quarrels, and they can still deal with all. So i just need to learn more from others. I will just need to be more skillful in dealing with this kind of behavior, and i won't blame anyone or anything. If I cannot get better and feel better, it's my fault!"

Facing a traumatic accident?

"No problem. No big deal! Many people have to live with even worse tragedies, and they can still overcome all! So I just need to learn more from others, and I won't blame anyone or anything. I will just need to get more skills, deal with the hardship, and cherish this precious life even without legs and hands. If I cannot feel better and get better, it's my fault!"

Facing a dreadful breakup?

"No problem. No big deal! Many people have to live with even worse incidents, yet they can still deal with all. So I just need to learn more from others, and I won't blame anyone or anything. I will just need to relish this only life I have, even without the one I love. If I cannot feel better and get better, it's my fault!"

"Let me! Let me learn more and deal with all matters. Let me take responsibility for whatever that comes. Let me take charge of my own existence!

If I can't make it, it's my fault!"

Eventually, don't wish for peacefulness in life. Embrace the exact ache of your own fate, and wish that you know how to make the most of it!

Take responsibility, take control, then learn and grow. This may be the most crucial skill you'll truly need each day.

Hence, erase all distress,

Forget all sorrows,

Let go all mishaps,

And relish this whole life.

Get up!

Get back your courage,

Cherish this dear Soul,

And control your own thoughts.

Focus on what you possess.

Focus on what you're blessed.

Forget what you can't.

And do what you **CAN**!

Move on. MOVE ON!

8

THRIVING FROM DEFEATS

We are all failures – at least the best of us are.

- J. M. Barrie

Great challenges make life interesting; overcoming them makes life meaningful. It's how you deal with failure that determines your happiness and success.

- Anonymous

The only real mistake is the one from which we learn nothing.

- Henry Ford

Many days in life, you may get stuck.

Your job may get dull and tough.

People turn rough and rude.

Days last long, stressful.

Nights turn long, sleepless.

The black past keeps filling heart.

And the gray future keeps obsessing soul.

…

It feels as if bad things just kept coming,

As if worse things would just pop up.

And that you'd never get free

To enjoy this life,

To ignite this heart,

And leave a mark on this world.

It feels like a dead-end, a blind alley, an eternal abyss.

But is it truly so?

Fortunately not!

No matter what happens, you can always find out a way to appease your heart. And importantly, you can always remind yourself that everyone has their own dark times in life.

They feel sad,

They feel angry,

Gloomy,

Lost,

And disappointed,

Just like you.

Everyone!

And these feelings won't just go away easily. At this point, **it is important to realize that your negative feelings are something universal, and that it is absolutely okay to have them.**

It is okay to be sad.

It is okay to be sick.

It is okay to be angry,

To be gloomy

Or disappointed.

It is okay to feel them. It is normal to have them.

It is abnormal not to!

So embrace them.

Knowing that it's just human nature to be negative sometimes,

That you share the basic emotions with billions of others,

And that you are totally OK and normal to be lost,

To be pained,

To be imperfect,

To be like everyone else!

And thank them.

Since no lessons could be learnt without having pains.

Since no growth could be reached without feeling bad.

And no changes could be made without tasting tortures.

A USEFUL HABIT

During difficult days, you can learn and grow tremendously by shaping new and useful habits. For a start, stop asking yourself negative questions and stop focusing on negative thoughts like:

"Why did this happen to me?"

"Why me? Why always me?"

"If..., then things would have been better."

Instead, ask yourself every time troubles come:

"Great! What lesson can i learn from this situation?

How can I find out its solution?

How can I deal with this one?

And how can I make the most of it?"

The truth is, no matter what really happens outside, your ultimate battle for a great life ahead always lies inside your own head.

It's the very **thoughts** and **beliefs** you have that can affect your day.

And it's the very **questions** you ask that can control your life path.

As such, it's critical to stop ruminating about your past life in mind.

*Focus your attention on the **solutions** and on the **lessons**, not the problems!*

Focus your thoughts on the right part – the part that you CAN control!

You feel sick? "I can now learn the lesson of health. What did i do wrong? I can now change my habits of eating, sleeping and exercising. I decide to take care of my health more than ever."

Hating your job? "I can now find the positive aspects of my job. How great can it help many people out there? How great can i contribute to my society and the lives of others? Alternatively, how can i find out a new way? How can i search for a better job?"

You feel angry? "I can now learn the lesson of communication. I can change my habits of speaking and listening. I can read more books and polish needed skills."

You feel unfulfilled? "I can now learn the lesson of gratitude. I can learn to appreciate everything I have. Besides, i can now learn the lesson of taking action. I can learn from exceptional people. And i can work towards my dreams instead of screaming loud."

Having some fears? "I can now learn the lesson of courage. I can learn to fix my imagination. I can learn to stare challenges on its face and keep moving forward."

Feeling lonely? "It's now time to learn the lesson of socializing and interacting with people. It's time to appreciate their good aspects and connect with them. It's time to learn the lesson of loving myself and loving my life. And it's time to accept the fact that it is okay to be lonely sometimes in life."

During difficult days, it'd be helpful if you could watch the news or read a good book. There're so many stories of people with cruel fates yet still succeed. They're the stories of courage and valor, of defeating dangers and adversities. They're the stories of making the most of what we do own.

THE VALUE OF HARDSHIPS

The point is, every negative feeling has its own message - the message hidden in your pain.

Every downfall has its own present - the present received by what you do afterwards.

In fact, hardships could potentially transform your feelings and viewpoints on the world. Hardships could potentially change your habits and reshape your entire life.

They could do so in a dramatic and powerful way.

Will your hardships make your life positive or negative?

Good or bad?

Better or worse?

It all depends on what lessons you get from the hard times.

And it all depends on what actions you take afterwards.

Sit still and complain? You could suffer more headaches and more heartaches.

Be brave, and take action? You could learn, you could grow, and you could make this life much brighter.

So think about your hard time. Learn something from it. And make your life even better from it.

Don't wish for a life without hardships. Accept every mistake and every headache in life, and wish that you can learn more from them all.

Meet Nelson Mandela.

Mr. Nelson struggled with his life for more than 27 years in prison before he was released in 1990. He fought for the anti-apartheid campaign, sacrificed his life for his people and became the very first democratically elected president of South Africa.

Imprisonment could detain his body but never his will.

In his own words:

"I learned that courage was not the absence of fear, but the triumph over it. The brave man is not he who does not feel afraid, but he who conquers that fear."

"It always seems impossible until it's done."

"Do not judge me by my successes, judge me by how many times I fell down and got back up again."

Enter the classic persistence of Abraham Lincoln.

Mr. Lincoln is probably one of the most famous examples of unwavering persistence. He was born into poverty, failed twice in business, had a nervous breakdown and suffered from depression. He was defeated eight times in elections before becoming president of the United States.

Abraham could have given up time and time again throughout his life, but he didn't. And the rewards for his persistence? - His great success that changed the course of history, and the admiration that generations have for him.

Meet Thomas Edison.

Thomas was an American inventor and businessman. He went through thousands of unsuccessful attempts to create a light bulb in his own lab. Give up? Not in his dictionary! He experimented again and again and again despite one failure after another.

And finally, he was successful at creating the first light bulb as he had always dreamt, and turned into the father of our modern light.

In his own words: "I have not failed. I've just found 10000 ways that won't work!"

The true value of a hardship is that, therefore, it can help you become teachable. Truly teachable!

Unless you make up your mind and decide to change much, it all will come back!

Hell or heaven, abyss or paradise, **it's all on you!**

"In every difficult situation is potential value. Believe this, then begin looking for it."

- Barbara De Angelis

The ultimate secret is that you can take everything happened as if it serves some great purposes. See everything happened as a precious gift in disguise as a trouble, and it was created by either your God or the Universe itself. Importantly, they are closely watching how wisely and bravely you respond to it. So never make your Self or your God disappointed!

After all, you won't know how great it is at the end of the road, until you decide to move on!

So just ask yourself:

What kind of negative feeling am i having right now?

What kinds of problems that have caused it?

What lessons can i learn?

And what changes can i make to get my life better?

Do that, NOW. The sooner you are aware of your own emotions, the faster you can glow and grow high.

The sooner you decide to change your habits and take needed actions, the faster you can strive and thrive well.

Do that **NOW!**

Find out what life brings to you.

And be truly living!

9

HOW TO FILL UP YOUR VITALITY?

Temptation is like a knife that may either cut the meat or the throat of a man; it may be his food or his poison, his exercise or his destruction.

- John Owen

True enjoyment comes from activity of the mind and exercise of the body; the two are ever united.

- Wilhelm von Humboldt

Health is the vital principle of bliss, and exercise, of health.

- James Thomson

Energy is an important piece of the Living Great puzzle.

When you feel energized, you're more likely to feel great. You're more eager to head for a new day, and you're more ready to face every challenge.

When you feel tired, you're more likely to be lousy. You're more likely to be overly stressed, and thus more likely to collapse under the pressure of life.

By discarding harmful habits and obtaining better ones, fortunately, you can dramatically improve your energy level. And with it, a better quality of life might follow.

Here are some important aspects that you should work on:

EXERCISING

Exercise drastically increases your excitement and energy level. Regular exercise helps release endorphins which serve to excite and enhance your mood. What's more, exercise remarkably improves your sleeping, organs' functions, memory, immunity, and affects the biochemistry of every living cell in a powerful and positive way. It's like a lubricant, a catalyst that boosts the living machinery of your entire body.

As such, spend at least 15 minutes each day to do some vigorous exercises. At first, you may find it lazy and busy to start. But hey, don't let that lazy voice inside control your whole life! It's extremely important to do exercise every day to make it an established habit.

Think about this: it takes us only 15 minutes each day to increase our mood, our life quality and working capacity, dramatically! Indeed, it's no different from a magic pill.

So what are we waiting for?

SLEEPING

Sleeping is an important mechanism to get rid of most metabolic toxins produced in the brain. In fact, when you sleep, your brain cells shrink and facilitate the drainage of those toxic substances. Without enough sleep, those toxins would mess up with your brain's ability to control the whole body. As a result, you would get tired and would not be able to think effectively. In the long term, moreover, a lack of sleep could be extremely devastating to your whole body, immunity and mind.

As such, try your best to get enough sleep each day. If you must wake up and go to work early, make sure you turn off the light timely at night. After that, switch off your phone and other distractions that can attract your attention before sleeping time.

Creating a proper environment this way to support your sleeping is supremely important. It is indeed a critical factor to have a good night. It's a must!

And crucially, it's always better if you can **match your sleeping time to the natural circadian rhythm**. Most importantly, try your best not to wake up too late in the morning, since doing so would likely make you feel tired, depressed and stressed out. Your own body and mind would most likely struggle between your sleeping habit and the natural instinct embedded within, and they would probably get devastated in the long run.

EATING

Proper eating provides you the ultimate source of energy needed for your whole day. As such, make sure you have a high amount of fruits and water, as well as a moderate amount of carbohydrates and proteins each day.

Also, avoid eating too much fried foods and fast foods, which slow down your own digestion, and may contain toxic substances which are extremely damaging to your body and mind.

So pay close attention to what you eat and what you drink. And don't ever let those harmful temptations defeat your will!

AWARENESS

To level up in life, you've got to carefully evaluate every habit you have, and spend proper time to develop better ones.

Crucially, spend 15 minutes each day to supervise your whole life. Determine what you should focus on, what you'll need to discard, and what you'll need to improve.

Use this important time to detect your life plan's weaknesses, and figure out proper ways to refine it.

In reality, this may be the most important time of the day. When you're fully aware of your life plan's strengths and weaknesses, you can know if your present habits are taking your way astray, and you can thus redirect its course to the right path. **Without spending decent time reflecting on your own path, you may end up being exceedingly far from the very life you wish.**

As such, spend your time to realize what you've possibly done wrong and what you'll need to improve. You can take a break and do it, right now.

Don't wait until it is too late!

TAKING ACTION

Finally and most importantly, it is your very action that really matters. Knowledge is of no use if you don't start taking action. After all, knowledge alone can't take you real far. It's only action that can take you further.

So devise a decent plan for your whole life. And start taking action, bit by bit each day. Shape all necessary habits, and start working toward your dreams.

You're planning to start sleeping at 10 p.m? First, you should set an alarm clock at 9h30, RIGHT AWAY! When the bell starts ringing, you should switch off the light, then turn off your internet and smartphone immediately.

Or if you're planning to take care of your health by doing exercise regularly, you should set an alarm, RIGHT AWAY! Prepare your shoes and other things needed to urge you when the moment comes!

The point is, it's your immediate action **RIGHT NOW** that can motivate and strengthen your resolve. It's your immediate action **RIGHT NOW** that ultimately truly matters!

So don't be hesitating.

And don't be overthinking!

Just act!

Just do it!

NOW, or NEVER!

Eventually, you must take care of your own health, and you must take care of your energy level. After all, you cannot strive toward your goals without enormous energy, and you cannot work toward your dreams without tremendous vigor.

As such, think of a concrete plan to fill up your vitality from now on. To face all challenges and fight against all headaches, you'll need it. To win the game of life and fight like a warrior, you'll need it even more. A lot of it indeed!

So carefully design your life to preserve your good health and maintain your good shape. Because ultimately, this life is not a one-day journey. This life is long, really long.

And it's indeed the greatest marathon.

10

THIS PRECIOUS MOMENT

You must live in the present, launch yourself on every wave, find your eternity in each moment. Fools stand on their island opportunities and look toward another land. There is no other land, there is no other life but this.

- Henry David Thoreau

I have realized that the past and future are real illusions, that they exist in the present, which is what there is and all there is.

- Alan Watts

Children have neither a past nor a future. Thus they enjoy the present, which seldom happens to us.

- Jean de La Bruyère

Many times in life, we immerse in sadness.

Nights after nights,
We revive our past,
With heartaches and tears,
With fears and darkness,
With mishaps and dismay.

Days after days,
Fear the way ahead,
And let pain conquer.

We ignore the only thing that really matters: The Present
We ignore the greatness of being alive, right NOW!

What happened last year, last week, last hour
Is already memory.
What'll happen next hour, next week, next year
Is still unknown.

The Past is just there,
And let you turn tough
To laugh at danger
And challenge darkness.

Lost loves can teach us
The path to compassion,

The lesson of sympathy,

Of forgiving and cheerfulness.

Lost lives can teach us

The lesson of loving,

Of caring and adoring

Every little thing.

Every pain - a gift.

Every loss - a present.

The lessons given

To help you flourish.

The Future is there,

And is yet unfold,

To be seen and expected,

To be tried and experimented.

Coz worries and fears

Are mere imaginations.

Each day you worry

Is another day lost.

Each second you panic

Is a second ruined.

Regretting that past

Fretting that future

Is a life in vain.

The ultimate moment

That you can get free

That you can truly live

Is just **This Present,**

Every hour,

Every minute,

Every second passing by

SAVOR THE WAY

What if

You lived in the past,

Traumatized by its life,

With sleepless nights and aching heart,

What would you get?

What if

You **thanked for your past,**

For the lessons it brings,

For the daring it constructs,

That made you stronger,

And got on with life?

What if

You lived the future,

Feared by disasters,

And worried by failures,

What would you get?

And if

You **planned the future,**

Performed all hard works,

One by one,

Step by step,

With no doubt or dread,

With no fret or fear,

What would you get?

What if

You **lived this present,**

Forgot destinations,

And smiled with the journey,

Relished what you'll do

And not what you'll get?

And if

You **lived each second,**

Cherished each moment,

Threw away heartaches,

And thanked for each day you have.

Then enjoyed

Every meal,

Every breath,

Every sip of wine,

Every sight,

Every step,

Every color

…

What would you get?

A better day?

And **a better life**?

WHAT WOULD YOU CHOOSE?

ONE DAY, WE'LL ALL BE DUST

When I die,

My atoms will come undone.

I'll be space dust, once again.

The wind will carry me,

And scatter me everywhere,

Like dandelions in springtime.

I'll visit worlds and alien moons,

It will be so damn poetic-

Until I land on your sandwich.

- *Anonymous*

Every day, we are so busy with life's hassles, worries and business.

We stress out, and we complain. We forget to stop and enjoy our lives a little.

So often, we cling on the pains of the past, regretting and mourning for the very things that we once possessed.

So often, we aren't satisfied with our own lives. We want more to come. We keep ourselves from being happy and cheery until achieving the thing we wish. Achieved, and we wish for more. And more. And even more.

So often, we hold negative feelings towards woeful events and cruel people out there. They disrespect us, they mistreat us, and they hurt us so much.

We tend to forget that, ultimately,

Everyone on this planet will die.

And everything in this life will be lost.

Forever!

We possess nothing in the long term. We possess nothing to fear losing. And we possess nothing to worry about so much.

As such, don't linger the pain of losing someone or something in life. And while it's hurtful to lose the one you love, it's important to remind yourself that eventually, one way or another, that thing or that person would cease to exist. It is therefore your mission to continue living, savoring this life, and keeping them in heart. In knowing that one day, you might rejoin them in the wind and dust. And maybe one day, you'd rejoin them in the afterlife.

What's more, don't waste your precious time for anxiety and worries of the future. Remind yourself that every struggle, every problem will sooner or later perish. Every mistake, every hardship will sooner or later die out. They simply play an natural part of every single life. They simply appear, grow and vanish with this endless time.

Much like everything else.

As such,

You don't need to be burdened with thoughts.

You don't need to take things so seriously,

And worry so much every day.

Just let go of the thought of wanting more in life. And stop obsessing yourself with the things that you can't have.

Coz you're still your Soul without them all.

And if you hate someone or something in life, think about this:

Everyone and everything you don't like will sooner or later vanish. It all will sooner or later die out, turning into dust and oblivion.

As such, what good does it do to keep negative attitude towards people instead of accepting whoever they are?

What good does it do to get obsessed with their faults and mistakes instead of seeing the good sides in them, and finding a better solution?

And what good does it do to poison yourself with anger and hatred, towards this very dust and sand?

Imagine that tomorrow, everything you see will be burnt into ashes, and that everyone you know will all evaporate. With that sight in mind, you can now smile and forgive other people. You can now treat them with all the kindness you've got. You can now relive and appreciate every little thing in life. You can now jump high with excitement and savor this beautiful day.

In knowing that ultimately, everything won't be around for much longer.

"Beginning today, treat everyone you meet as if they were going to be dead by midnight. Extend to them all the care, kindness and understanding you can muster, and do it with no thought of any reward. Your life will never be the same again."

– Og Mandino

And eventually, your life will be lost too.

Forever!

You will die.

You will vanish.

You will miss this very day.

And you will miss this very life.

You will miss every little one, and every little thing in it!

Ultimately, this life is short.

Really short!

It is delicate.

And indeed precious!

So ask yourself:

What's the point of burdening your mind with ordinary matters, and losing the chance of living great?

What's the point of misspending your life for yesterday's troubles or tomorrow's worries, and neglecting to enjoy every second you've owned?

What's the point of wanting more, and more, and even more in life, while forgetting to appreciate every little thing you've got?

Ultimately, you have nothing to lose, and you have nothing to fear in this life. You have one and only one chance to breathe and relish this very existence. So start putting all darkness of the past aside. Throw worries of the future into oblivion. Live in the moment. Live in the second! And savor this day as if it were your very last.

Drink it! Breathe it! Immerse in it!

For this ONLY chance!

11

DIFFICULT PEOPLE AND SITUATIONS: AN APPROACH

Empathy is seeing with the eyes of another, listening with the ears of another and feeling with the heart of another.

- William James

Knowing your own darkness is the best method for dealing with the darkness of other people.

– Carl Jung

When I get ready to talk to people, I spend two thirds of the time thinking what they want to hear and one third thinking about what I want to say.

- Abraham Lincoln

Do you often have aching headaches when your troubles come?

Or struggle with people and their behaviors, and get obsessed with being right?

When it comes to dealing with difficult people and circumstances, there are eventually two crucial problems to solve.

First, there is the internal battle, the "What I Feel" in the face of the headache. It's the incessant battle to stay in peace and calmness. It's the persistent fight to get away from anger and negativity. And it's the endless struggle to regain your inner control of the situation.

Second, there is the external battle, the "What I Do" in response to a circumstance or a behavior. It's the execution of your plan to deal with the matter at hand, and it's the action you do to change the consequences of your situation.

As often, it is the solution of your external problems that brings you your desired outcomes, and it is the solution of your internal troubles that brings you your desired feelings.

The truth is, while your external struggle is often complicated, intricate, and requires a whole bunch of life experience and communication skills to resolve, it is the internal battle that's more important and more difficult to learn. Your internal feelings will, ultimately, decide the quality of your life more than any external outcome. And what's more, controlling your feelings first can also help tremendously in the acceptance and solution of your outside struggles.

As such, for this important section, let's first talk about our internal struggle and its significance. Let's find out some great and useful methods to control this internal warfare.

THE FAILURE OF EXPECTATIONS

Do you find it easier to forgive your pets than many people?

And do you often have more tolerance for most children than for adults?

Rest assured that you're not alone. In fact, most of us do behave that way. Why? Because ultimately, you expect your pets and most children to be naïve and innocent. They are supposed to be young and inexperienced. Children are expected to make mistakes, to say silly words and to be forgiven many times. As such, you may feel okay with their mistakes and annoyance. You may feel okay with their insolence time and time again.

Let's pause for a moment, and ponder upon that.

In fact, it's not the behavior of others that ultimately drives you mad: it's the expectation you have for them that actually brings you pain. For a moment, just compare your expectations for all people who you don't like, versus your expectations for your own pets and for children. Do you feel bad with people because you expect too much from them?

As such, if you often have problems dealing with people, maybe your expectations for them are just too high: you expect people to be nice and perfect, you expect people to be fair and respectful, you expect them to adhere to the "Should" standards that you create in mind? And once they fail to do so, you become angry, disappointed and frustrated. You're drowned in an ocean of hatred and resentment. And you just fall into a relentless trap of negativity that you created for your own mind.

The ultimate solution is, perhaps, to have lower expectations for other people.

For a start, let's learn to give and help without hoping to get back. Engage people and expect every possible scenario. Expect less kindness, less respect, less listening and understanding from others.

And expect that most people are having a very bad day. Expect that they'll screw up today by saying or doing something stupid. Expect them all to be naive and make mistakes often. Expect them all to be in need of your acceptance. And expect many to be selfish, guilty and offensive from time to time.

After all, there are various types of people and circumstances in this world. Good and bad, haste and calm, devils and angels. As such, **don't expect perfection. Expect strange, weird, and unbelievable situations.**

Importantly, let's learn to accept and appreciate people the way they are born, unconditionally. Accept and learn to deal with their behaviors, and treat them with your acceptance and understanding. Treat them the way you treat a child who's learning his way to grow up.

But what if you've tried your best and still can't deal with their behaviors? You may just need to feel your inner peace and stay totally calm first, then just forgive them all and walk far away.

By doing so, you can always be in control of your emotion.

EXPECT THE WORST

Having proper expectations would, therefore, help you stay cool and calm in confronting the situation at hand. It would let you be in total control of your feelings and reactions, and it would let you be in total control of yourself!

In contrast, having improper expectations would make yourself passive and reactive to anything that happens. If things turned out to be unexpected, negative feelings would come up to ravage your inner peace, and you'd be trapped in an angry and out-of-control state.

Would you then be able to resolve the situation at hand, or would you just put more flame to its smoldering fire?

The point is, the more you expect to deal with the worst troubles, the less surprising this life will unfold. And the more you prepare yourself for the worst scenarios, the more control you will get over the matter.

The more ideal you expect this world to be, the more heartaches and headaches it will throw at you.

The more **nature-compatible** you expect this world to be, the more cheerfulness and happiness it will serve you.

That's how life works!

THE DAILY PRACTICE

As such, having proper expectations for the world can help you conquer difficult feelings and situations of everyday life.

Before dealing with someone or something coming, just pause for a second. Try to visualize the worst-case scenarios that might happen, and how you should deal with them. Say, your boss might fire you, your love might hurt you, the crowd might shame you, the dog might bite your leg, or the weather might ruin your day.

Afterwards, familiarize yourself with the negative feelings of the scenarios over time. Embrace it all! Be brave to face anything, and think about how you should deal with them.

Don't wait for life to happen and react to it.

Don't be reactive. Be proactive!

Think about it. If you can always expect and prepare for the worst, you'll waste no energy stressing yourself. And if you come up with a good plan for anything that could happen, you'll waste no time heartbreaking when the storms of life finally lands in your path.

Imagine it.

If you embrace the worst that might happen, will you be taken aback by unexpected events?

And if you turn brave to face it all, will you fear shame, anger, disappointment and frustration anymore?

Expect the hell.

And embrace the hellish.

Hope for the best.

But prepare for the worst!

Always!

THE SECOND WEAPON IN HAND

All hostility, racism, contempt and hatred in this world ultimately come from this word:

EGO.

The ultimate source of most relationship's sorrows comes from the individuality of each individual - the Ego. It's the tendency of each individual to bias his thoughts and actions. It's the tendency of each individual to defend his will, blame people, and favor himself over others in the struggle to survive and prosper.

After all, we feel it easier to sympathize with ourselves than with someone else, and to find excuses for our wrongdoings than for others'. Is it not?

The lesson learnt is that, therefore, we should stop judging people.

Every one of us has a different genetic predisposition, a different environment and condition of living. Everyone has a different life direction that shape their personality, habits, strengths and weaknesses. Every one of us is different! It is therefore subjective to judge people, and guess who they really are from our point of view. It is partial to do so.

And who knows, maybe if we were in their situation, we would become an even worse person! Maybe if we were in their shoes, we would have committed more sins and made more mistakes than they did. Maybe we would even make it worse. Much worse!

What's more, we should also eliminate the obsession with being right all the time.

All events we experienced in life and the personality we get often let us create the "Behavior Standards" that we use to judge and evaluate others. It is helpful that some of those standards, say, our social laws are necessary to maintain the stability and structure of our society, and they should be considered as proper standards by everyone.

Most of the time, however, our inner standards are extremely personal and subjective, and there is no clear-cut boundary of what is right and what is wrong. What you consider right and appropriate may sound completely weird and awful to others. What you consider noisy and lousy may sound perfectly nice and delightful to them. It may seem wrong to you to ignore a friend's call and never call back, while it's okay for others if they're busy and forget. It may seem okay for you to cross the red light sometimes, or to criticize someone harshly when they mess up. For many others, however, it's not acceptable to do so.

After all, people do things "wrong" again and again. All of us do! All of us are different! Let's expect that.

And it's also a good idea to see life from others' perspective.

Consider seeing things from their own points of view, and see how different they are from you. See how they are "wrong" from your perspective, and how you are "wrong" from theirs. See how conflict can arise, and how you may reconcile it.

Question yourself if you are "wrong" from time to time. Maybe you are!

Question yourself if you do things "wrong" from time to time. Maybe you do!

AN EFFECTIVE APPROACH

Therefore, one simple solution to the problem of dealing with people is that we should just SPEAK IT OUT. People wouldn't know what you expect from them unless you told them. People wouldn't know if their world and your world do clash if you kept silent. And they wouldn't know what you like or dislike if you didn't speak it out.

After all, they're not telepathic!

So tell others what you think and what you want. But do it with skills and grace. Do it in an elegant way.

And it's necessary that you ask them what they think you should do too. It's important to know what they expect from others. It's important to listen and see their private points of view.

After that, work for a solution or an agreement of what to do with them, and what to expect in a specific situation. The more **detailed and unequivocal** the solution is, the less frustration and disappointment a conflict can inflict upon you!

In short, to approach people more effectively, it's best to have less criticism and less prejudice. It's best to find common grounds and accept differences as much as possible.

What's more, it's crucial to be open to new rules and "standards" inside other people, and work with them towards a common solution. It is critical to recognize what's wrong with our own plan and approach, instead of always finding faults outside.

And if any difficult situation arises, you can always control your inside and find your inner peace first.

This doesn't mean that you should always tolerate and get along with every bad behavior. It's toxic to do so. This is to say that you should feel calm, empathetic, and be in total control of your feelings first. It is better to approach any situation while being calm and composed first, isn't it?

And after that, you can start your plan to resolve the outside situation.

Learn and execute effective strategies to deal with all behaviors. Books, internet, friends and family can help you in this aspect. They have all kinds of valuable experiences that can help you learn and grow each day.

So today, let's start being cool, calm and collected, in any situation.

Let's Shape A New Self!

12

WHAT IF THIS WAS YOUR LAST DAY?

Dream as if you'll live forever. Live as if you'll die today.

- James Dean

And in the end, it's not the years in your life that counts. It's the life in your years.

- Abraham Lincoln

To change one's life: Start immediately. Do it flamboyantly. No exceptions.

- William James

December 21, 2012,

This day was the end of the Mayan calendar, and it would be the end of the world as many had believed. Still, i was sitting on a couch doing homework, scratching my head as time went by. All of a sudden, i heard "the end of the world" by Skeeter Davis, coming from somewhere far away.

"What a beautiful song!", I thought. It made me excited. Truly excited!

And it kept me pondering upon life and death.

What if today was the end of the world?

What if today was the last day of my life?

What would i do?

Questions and revelations just occupied my mind. If today was the last day of my life, maybe I would go out and savor it. I would eat delicious foods and breathe this fresh air for the last time. I would meet my dearest ones and have laughs. I would look at the sky and yell out real loud. I would cherish and relish every second as if it were my very heart.

I would make this last day the most memorable and unforgettable one.

And gradually, i could appreciate the value of various things that i'd never noticed before. Gradually, each meal, each taste turned into something sweet. Each sight, each breath turned into a miracle.

It was like a different life.

The point is, as we appreciate the day and savor everything in it, joy exudes.

As we appreciate the things we have that many people don't, we feel complete.

And as we don't suffer the hardships that millions of others do, we feel so much happier.

We feel troubled with life because we're too serious with it. We focus too much on the persons that we can't please, on the very things that we can't possess, and on the matters that we can't control.

We immerse so much in our own headaches and heartaches, and think that it's the end of the world.

We tend to forget that our hardships are nothing abnormal. We tend to forget that every one of us gets a slap in the face from time to time.

No exception!

And we tend to forget that many others are suffering more. Much more than we do!

A HELPFUL APPROACH

During difficult times, let us watch a survival or an apocalyptic movie. It could work magic and change your whole perspective. It could change your appreciation of the life you have, and get you out of the negative thinking that you're enduring.

Imagine you were in the movie "2012". If you involved yourself in the burning fire of the world, if you were running away from looming disasters, and striving to take your last gasp on Earth, how would you feel about your current headache? Would you find it less grave? Would you find it less significant?

Let yourself be in "Hacksaw Ridge". When you engaged yourself in a threatening situation, of bullets and fire, of life and death, of shackles and chains, how would you feel about your current situation? Would you smile at ordinary fears and live more bravely? Would you let go of every petty hate and live more in love?

Imagine yourself in "Cast Away". When you involved yourself in an agonizing circumstance, of loneliness and tears, of fear and thirst, of blood and pain, how would you feel about your current heartache? Would you stop hurting yourself with your loss and pain, strain and distress, sadness and despair? Would you love yourself and cherish your life to the utmost?

THE KEYS OF LIVING

It is during the darkest moments that you realize one point important: **that the most basic things like breathing, eating, talking, smiling are those that matter most.** Those are the things that bring you the most out of living. Those are the things that you cannot exist without! Not the house, not the car, not the awesome achievement, nor the glorious road filled with roses in your dreams.

The most basic things that we possess are the primary keys of life.

Other things are just secondary.

This doesn't mean that you shouldn't care about success or achievement.

This means that you should be happy and appreciate your keys first, that you should forget and eliminate all worries, that you should defy all mishaps and get in love with this life.

And after that, you should gradually think of a concrete plan to reach for your dream. And you should determinedly take a massive amount of action to achieve it.

IMAGINING DEATH

Imagining and contemplating death is a powerful way of reshaping your life.

Confronting death, you could change your perspectives and priorities of life.

You could realize that you focused too much on the tiny headaches and heartaches of life, and forgot to enjoy its most important aspects.

You could relish various delights that you've taken for granted,

And thank for every little thing around.

You could fall in love with every sight,

Every step,

Every meal,

Every breath,

Every color,

…

Contemplating death is a powerful way of life. It brings out the awareness of loving, of living, and of being alive.

More than ever!

Imagine today as the last day of your life. A big asteroid might strike. An unfortunate accident might happen. A super volcano might erupt. A nuclear war might begin. And a thin life might be lost.

Imagine it. Immerse in it.

And ask yourself:

Would my problems and headaches matter anymore?

Would i still be afraid to move forward?

Would i still fear any distress or failure?

Would i occupy myself with anger, sadness and negativity?

Or would i defy all petty matters?

And savor life's wonders for the last time?

Ultimately, our life is precious.

And our life is short.

Really short!

So let's enjoy it.

Don't care so much about how others may shame you. Don't care so much about how others may hurt you.

Coz you are living your life, not anyone else's!

So do the things you like.

Find out your passions.

Find out what you love!

And don't hold back your elation.

Be a little silly.

Be a little crazy.

And be excited with this life.

Jump into it with a song you love!

Dance inside it like everyone's cheering.

And adore your laughs as if this day were the last.

Your life is short. Really short! And with each passing day, it comes closer to an end.

Your life is short, and delicate! You may never know exactly when you'll leave this world. Maybe next year, next month, or maybe today! We all may never know that.

Hence, take a deep breath. Walk a few steps. And relish this very day. Don't waste the only life you have for past pains and future worries. Don't waste the only life you have for blaming and complaining.

Coz this day will never happen again. So make the most of it!

A DAILY REMINDER

Each morning waking up, feel how great it is that you're being alive.

And tell yourself, "Today may be my last day on this planet. And i'm gonna live it full out for the last time!"

Every day, you have the chance to be worthy,

To feel lucky,

To thank for your food and water,

And to savor the life that many people wish for.

Every day, you have the chance to feel the thrilling juice of loving, of living, and of being alive inside your dear heart.

Every day, you have the chance

To live a life out of this ordinary.

Every day, you have the chance

To live a life extraordinarily.

The Life Is Yours!

mp3.zing.vn/bai-hat/ZW6ZZE8C.html

CONCLUSION

Dear friends, i would like to thank you so much for taking a look at this book. And i genuinely hope that you'd love it as much as I do.

If you found this book inspiring, you could recommend and share it to other people in need. It'd be my great honor.

And finally, I wish you a happy and fulfilling life ahead. May courage and strength be always with you.

Let's make this day, this life, this me and this you unforgettable.

The Life Is Ours!

CONTACT ME

It would be great to hear about your own life stories and experiences. Please contact me at: thanducthinh123@gmail.com

Made in the USA
Middletown, DE
07 December 2018